Drama and Theatre Studies

China:
entenary Celebration
well Swortzell, editors

ics of the Puppet:
rical Art

briel

ssee Williams's *A Streetcar Named Desire*:
luralism
tor

erarchy:
n the United States

nerican Drama:
Criticism, 1746–1915
ditor

ir Experiences and Careers

d Festival Theatre

irector:
and Performance Interpretations
Sidney Berger, advisory editor

w and the Socialist Theatre

ing:
es for Brecht, Ionesco, Pinter and Shepard

ollection of Critical Essays

JUN(

THI

Recent Titles in
Contributions in

Eugene O'Neill in
An International C
Haiping Liu and L

Toward an Aesthe
Puppetry as a The
Steve Tillis

George Sand's *Ga*
Gay Manifold

Confronting Tenn
Essays in Critical I
Philip C. Kolin, ed

Challenging the Hi
Collective Theatre
Mark S. Weinberg

The Dawning of A
American Dramati
Jürgen C. Wolter,

The Actor Speaks:
Actors Discuss The
Joan Jeffri, editor

Richard Wagner an
Simon Williams

Playwright versus I
Authorial Intention
Jeane Luere, editor

George Bernard Sh
Tracy C. Davis

Playwrights and Ac
Acting Methodolog
James H. McTeagu

Israel Horovitz: A C
Leslie Kane, editor

JUNG'S ADVICE TO THE PLAYERS

A Jungian Reading of Shakespeare's Problem Plays

Sally F. Porterfield

Contributions in Drama and Theatre Studies, Number 57

GREENWOOD PRESS
Westport, Connecticut • London

Library of Congress Cataloging-in-Publication Data

Porterfield, Sally F.
Jung's advice to the players : a Jungian reading of Shakespeare's problem plays / Sally F. Porterfield.
p. cm.—(Contributions in drama and theatre studies, ISSN 0163–3821 ; no. 57)
Includes bibliographical references and index.
ISBN 0–313–29305–8 (alk. paper)
1. Shakespeare, William, 1564–1616—Knowledge—Psychology. 2. Jung, C. G. (Carl Gustav), 1875–1861—Views on literature. 3. Shakespeare, William, 1564–1616—Tragicomedies. 4. Shakespeare, William, 1564–1616. Hamlet. 5. Archetype (Psychology) in literature. 6. Psychoanalysis and literature. I. Title. II. Series.
PR3065.P67 1994
822.3'3—dc20 94–5150

British Library Cataloguing in Publication Data is available.

Library of Congress Catalog Card Number: 94–5150
ISBN: 0–313–29305–8
ISSN: 0163–3821

First published in 1994

Greenwood Press, 88 Post Road West, Westport, CT 06881
An imprint of Greenwood Publishing Group, Inc.

Printed in the United States of America

The paper used in this book complies with the Permanent Paper Standard issued by the National Information Standards Organization (Z39.48–1984).

10 9 8 7 6 5 4 3 2 1

Contents

Acknowledgments

I am grateful to Charlotte Spivack, for showing me that Jung and Shakespeare are a natural pairing, and for her unfailing support in this effort. Thanks also to Christine Herold for her work on the archetype of the spirit in *Hamlet*, and to John Hunt, Dick Trousdell, Joe Donahue, Bob Keefe, and Charles Taylor, for their help and advice.

Special thanks go to Ann Bliss, for her loving wisdom and for convincing me that it's never too late. Finally, thanks and love to Dean, Annie, Jane, and Matt, for everything.

Sally Porterfield

JUNG'S ADVICE TO THE PLAYERS

Chapter I

Introduction

It is through art that mankind has always attempted to reconcile his inner experience with the world outside himself. From the Altamira cave paintings to Jackson Pollock's Abstract Expressionism, we can see the record of that search in the visual arts. Embedded in our music, our architecture, and our literature are the trail markings of that inner journey, what might be regarded, in Jungian terms, as the history of the collective western psyche.

Carl Gustav Jung, one of the world's greatest travelers of inner space, that other "undiscovered country" showed us that we might indeed return from its bourn the richer and wiser. And so, like explorers, we shall attempt to follow Jung's charts and maps of those inner regions in order to see how well they serve as guides to some of our most tantalizing mysteries, Shakespeare's problem plays, defined here as the three "bitter comedies," and *Hamlet*.

The extraordinary power, the numinosity of great art stems from its ability to speak to the unconscious, that part of us which Jung tells us communicates not in words, but in symbols.[1] Theatre, which combines verbal and visual arts, works on both levels in a particularly potent way. The words, which appeal to the conscious mind by their intellectual, emotional, or aesthetic content, also speak to the unconscious, calling up personal and archetypal associations the conscious mind cannot recognize but can experience, sometimes in bewilderingly powerful ways.

It seems pertinent here, since we are dealing with Shakespeare, the Western world's greatest dramatist, to discuss briefly the phenomenon of drama as a form from a Jungian perspective. Theatre historians present a compelling case for their art, which encompasses all the others, as the most ancient of all. Primitive man, in his first attempts at communication,[2] might well have acted out some great event, such as the hunt, with one actor taking the role of the animal and others reenacting their own role as hunters. Such conjectures are bolstered by what we know from anthropologists' studies of later primitive societies. But even prior to language, back in the dimmest mists of prehistory, we can imagine that such attempts at communication took place. Later, as the storyteller became the first author/playwright, his words might have been illustrated and enhanced by visual recreation.

But the deepest roots of Western theatre as we know it are religious. Our knowledge is based mainly on the hieroglyphics and artifacts of ancient Egypt, which depict rituals of the death and rebirth of Osiris, the god whom scholars have suggested may be the precursor of Dionysus. From the fifth century B.C., the love-hate relationship between organized religion and theatre has paralleled the death and rebirth drama that Jung regarded as one of our deepest archetypal expectations.[3]

Try as it would, the church was unable to kill Dionysus permanently. Condemned to live underground for over five hundred years by the early Christian church, he emerged again, not in the marketplace but in the church itself, as a dramatization of Christ's rebirth in the *Quem Queritis Trope*. From that time on, of course, he has grown weak each time Apollo becomes the prude or the zealot, but he is always born again when society most needs him. Sometimes he appears as a licentious rogue, as during the Restoration, sometimes as a passionate crusader or gentle humanist, as in the late nineteenth century works of Ibsen and Chekhov.

What is this power the drama holds for so many? From where does the magic emanate that suffuses this art form and elevates it into something very closely resembling a religious calling for so many people? If we accept the premise that great literary characters derive their power from the archetypes they invoke, then we can take that belief one step further. In drama, the power is intensified by the merger of character and actor, which brings the archetype, quite literally, to life. Perhaps after all, this is the power that enthralls most in theatre, the fusion of unconscious and conscious reality, not on a page or on canvas, but in the flesh. The merger might be regarded as part of that alchemical process which Jung believed to be a symbolic search for the self. The word becomes flesh, and we realize that we are in the presence of the divine.

The debate about Shakespeare as literature versus drama will no doubt continue as long as there are combatants with sufficient passion and energy to endure. The emphasis of this work is firmly on the side of drama not only philosophically, but because an archetypal reading demands it. An understanding of dramatic literature from a Jungian standpoint can be of great assistance to the director or actor seeking ways for the play to speak visually.

The unconscious has no idea of time or place, but only of universal and eternal verities. Archetypal images can appear in the costume of any time or place and be equally recognizable to the unconscious. It is the conscious mind that needs some help in sorting them out, and that is where trends in the production of Shakespeare enter the picture.

We have returned in recent years to productions that are far closer to what we know about the originals than the elaborate epics that evolved out of late-nineteenth and early-twentieth-century realism. Minimalist sets and costumes which allow Shakespeare's words to do the work are common. For our purposes here, by far the most significant trend is toward multiracial, multiethnic casting, combined with antirealistic scenography of no particular time or place. Little imagination is needed to see some of these sets as dreamscapes peopled by figures from the unconscious.

Many productions, of course, have placed the plays in specific historical contexts. Thus, our century has seen *Hamlet* in black leather, in business suits, possibly even in drag. Not all of these efforts are happy, but the point they make is clear: Shakespeare's characters continue to fascinate us because they are as familiar as our own time, our own place, our own mind. Like time travelers, they can drop in anywhere and feel at home, because they are archetypal.

As for the choice of material here it was Frederick S. Boas who first described this group of four works as Shakespeare's "problem plays," borrowing the term from the then popular thesis plays of such writers as Ibsen and Shaw, whose work dealt with social problems. Although some subsequent critics have included only the three bitter comedies, *Measure for Measure, All's Well That Ends Well,* and *Troilus and Cressida,* in the designation, Boas included *Hamlet* too as the ultimate problem play, the puzzle that has intrigued so many for so long.[4] Charles Boyce provides a particularly succinct statement concerning the group:

> Once we understand that moral issues are the plays' 'raison d'etre,' we can adjust to the symbolic aspects of character and the allegorical nature of some of the plotting. The extent to which moral questions are stressed makes clear their importance to Shakespeare, and his refusal to provide easy answers to them makes them particularly potent. Shakespeare recognizes, as always, the complexity of life and the difficulty in making moral judgments. The capacity of these plays to disturb causes us to be more engaged in these questions; we become aware of the need to strive after ideals, to pursue and believe in virtue even though we, like the figures in the plays, may not fully achieve it.[5]

The three dark comedies seem particularly apt for study now, in these last years of a century that has seen such enormous changes, particularly in the context of relations between and the role definitions of men and women. Jung, despite the conservative, sexist bias that pervaded his society and his own thinking, has much to say to any age about the ways in which we all need to accept our own sexuality and our contra-sexual characteristics. When we view the plays through Jung's lens, perhaps we are better able to understand how Shakespeare came to terms with those same issues through the genius of his art.

Much of the "problem" caused by these three plays has centered around their categorization as "comedies," a term that, despite its checkered past, raises certain expectations in both reader and audience member. They are certainly closer to our contemporary black comedy than to the relatively sanitary New Comedy form that has pervaded most English dramatic literature since the Restoration.

In our own century dramatists like Samuel Beckett, Harold Pinter, Edward Albee, Joe Orton, Sam Shepard, and Christopher Durang owe a debt of gratitude to their Renaissance forbears, who, unconcerned with unities or rules, wrote about life as they saw and experienced it. The down and dirty that makes up much of life can be very funny, and often we must choose laughter instead of tears in order to survive.

Martyn Green, one of the great English Savoyards of the twentieth-century, was a master of Gilbert and Sullivan's patter songs and an artist of unequaled physical agility. As Ko-Ko in *The Mikado*, probably his most famous role, his squirrel-like scamper straight up the side of a flat was the stuff of theatrical legend. At the peak of his career he lost a leg in a tragic elevator accident in his own Manhattan apartment building. The limb was amputated on the spot by a resident from one of the local hospitals. Green's life changed forever. He continued to perform, with amazing courage and ingenuity, but his constant companion was an everlasting reminder, the ache of his "phantom" limb.

Almost immediately after the accident Green became interested in black comedy as a path to survival. A hospital official came to his room with some papers to sign, giving permission for burial of the leg. Still in shock and pain, Green managed to answer with characteristic irony: "All right, I'll sign the papers, but I'll be goddammed if I'll go to the funeral."[6]

Perhaps it is with that kind of spirit that we should approach these plays, as a celebration of humanity's ability to laugh at its own pain and weep for its own happiness. Hamlet himself is the very embodiment of those qualities, of the glorious contradictions that make us human and all the richness that is to be found within this remarkable ephemeral machine.

Any attempt to approach Shakespeare from a critical point of view must be launched with considerable trepidation. We must be like the blind men and the elephant in our efforts to describe the complexity of this wonder. Various critical viewpoints need not be mutually exclusive, but rather should enhance our collective understanding of the material. Harold C. Goddard makes that point elegantly:

> And this [critical] process will continue to create what might be called the world's slowly growing portrait of Hamlet. Over the years the cairn of *Hamlet* criticism is more than any stone that has been thrown on it.[7]

The central concept of Jung's work was his theory of the individuation process, by which the ego reaches a stage of consciousness and identifies with the self, or the highest aspect of the individual's personality. In the course of a lifetime the individual must come to terms with all the various aspects of the psyche, or the personality, integrating all these disparate parts and working toward individuation or selfhood as the ultimate goal.

This process occurs to a greater or lesser extent universally, but Jung argues that civilized man, who has journeyed far from his primitive, unconscious beginnings, must reconcile those aspects of the unconscious and bring them to consciousness before he can accomplish this growth into the highest possible evolution of his own potential. Although no one ever reaches full individuation, the process of working toward that goal is what Jung regards as the individuation process.

These elements of the personality, according to Jung, come to consciousness at different times in life, sometimes taking on the characteristics of an autonomous complex and causing us to project them onto other individuals or situations until we can recognize them for what they are, a part of our own unconscious. These, then, are the archetypes of the collective unconscious, defined as:

> The inherited part of the psyche; structuring patterns of psychological performance linked to instinct; a hypothetical entity irrepresentable in itself and evident only through its manifestations.[8]

Thus, these contentless tendencies exist outside of time or space, manifesting themselves, like chameleons, in the colors of their environment and remaining always old and always new to each of us in our time. The most frequently discussed of these are the shadow, or that part of us which the persona suppresses, and the anima or animus, our contra-sexual side. We often project our own shadow on our enemy and our anima or animus on the object of our erotic desire, thus investing others with the contents of our own unconscious, rendering them numinous, or magical, in our eyes.

Other common archetypes are the father, the mother, the trickster, the hero, the spirit, the persona, the holy child, and a host of others, including not only figures but events, like death and rebirth. Many of these archetypes can be found over and over in myth and folktale, and thus have their literary roots deeply established within each culture. Although individual manifestations are culturally influenced, the basic patterns are easily recognizable.

In addition to his individuation process and the archetypes of the collective unconscious, Jung's personality types represent the most widely known portion of his work. Many, perhaps most people familiar with the terms are unaware that Jung developed the theory behind the introverted and extraverted personality types. In addition to these two main categories, Jung proposed that each individual also possesses the rational functions of thinking and feeling and the irrational faculties of intuition and sensation. Each of us has a dominant and an inferior function in each of the three categories. For example, a given individual might be extraverted with dominant thinking and sensation functions, introverted with dominant feeling and intuitive functions, or any combination of the three classifications. In individuation, we strive to bring these faculties into greater balance, although we usually retain our original bias toward one or the other. Either an individual or a society can become dangerously unbalanced and thus cripple further development or individuation.

A Jungian reading, like any psychological method, works on at least two levels. Viewed this way, occurrences in the plays constitute both actual and psychological events. Characters represent both themselves and archetypes from the collective unconscious. This cannot be stressed too strongly, since a failure to understand the liminal nature of this criticism results in too literal a reading and becomes reductive, rather than expansive.

The other cautionary note necessary here is a word about Renaissance drama as a form. Coming as it did close on the heels of the medieval world, drama of this period retains many elements of the mystery and morality plays. Shakespeare's characters, then, like those of his contemporaries, often retain their emblematic or allegorical character beneath a Renaissance cloak of individuality. Thus, we experience a richness of layering, most evident in an Iago as thinly disguised but chillingly sinister vice. Although most of Shakespeare's characters evidence this phenomenon in a much more subtle manner, the layering is there, nonetheless, and often contributes to the overwhelmingly archetypal associations they evoke.

In the process of viewing characters and events in this light, they are thrown into sharp relief as familiar components of the universal psychic drama. As reader, actor or director, we are able to find ways of clarifying and isolating vital elements of the whole. But this is simply the initial process, analogous to scales and exercises for a musician. Ultimately, all the separate pieces merge once more into the artistic whole. The alchemy of art produces a whole infinitely greater than the sum of its parts. Jung, for whom alchemy was symbolic of individuation, or selfhood, would surely agree with that analysis.

Each of the four plays centers around a specific critical axis, some broad hints at which are given in the chapter subtitles. *Measure for Measure* shows the effects of complete shadow suppression and the ways in which such unrealistic expectations can result in possession by those qualities we most want to avoid. *Hamlet* shares some of the same tendencies, but revolves mainly around the dissociation and trickster possession that result from the idealistic young prince's confrontation with the reality of his parents as fallible human beings. The trickster theme is also dominant in *All's Well,* providing an entirely new way of viewing Helena, as a trickster-savior figure. *Troilus and Cressida* differs from the other three plays in that it deals with the fixation of an entire society, rather than centering on one or two main characters. Here we see a reigning archetype that contrives to fix a whole society in the stage of the hero, thus preventing any further development toward maturity and individuation.

Thus, Jungian literary criticism works very much like the individuation process itself. By bringing to consciousness those textual elements that exist within our subconscious, we can integrate them and come closer to wholeness, both within ourselves and within the world. That is why we keep coming back to Shakespeare, because we see ourselves not just in that mirror he holds up to nature but through the looking glass, where the watchers within see their own version of the drama that they live through us.

Chapter II

Me and My Shadow: Enantiodromia in *Measure for Measure*

Cucullus non facit monachum
(V.i, 263)

Chronologically *Measure for Measure* falls last in the four year period between 1600 and 1604 that produced the body of work we propose to examine here. From a schematic point of view, however, it is logical to consider this play first, because it falls most clearly into the pattern of a classic, successful Jungian drama of individuation.

Viewed that way, many of the contradictions that so rankle our sense of justice begin to fall into place as a redressing of the universal inner drama. We recognize the ugliness as part of our own dark confusions, as Shakespeare's genius merges psychological and artistic reality.

Let us first introduce the characters, not quite in order of appearance, but in order of their importance in the individuation drama. That bothersome, tantalizing Duke of dark corners proclaims his sovereignty without doubt, as he claims both the first and last words in the play. He is the self, what James Kirsch refers to as "Shakespeare's Royal Self" in his book of that name.[1] Symbolically, the self appears in dreams or in art, as a king, a prince, a ruler of some sort. For three of these plays that becomes a very important issue, particularly in *Measure for Measure* and in *Hamlet*.

Even more significant perhaps, in the case of Duke Vincentio, is the fact that he furnishes the impetus for all the action. He, like an undercover Prospero, acts as a surrogate for the playwright himself within the play. Seen this way, his behavior takes on an entirely new character, but of that, more later.

Then what of Angelo, that arch hypocrite, who provides a model for all the self-deluding shams who hide their sensuality under the cloak of sanctimony? He is easy to recognize if we only look about us at some of his contemporary manifestations: the charismatic evangelist, the judgmental politician. Too often, those who seem too good to be true turn out to be just that. He is the persona divorced from psychological reality, an animated projection of false virtue who has ceased to know anything at all about his own humanity.

From a Jungian perspective, each of these plays revolves around a specific critical axis which, in this case, is possession by the persona. Angelo, in attempting to achieve an impossible perfection, experiences what Jung refers to as enantiodromia. Once the pendulum has reached its outer limits in one direction, it has nothing to do but return. Bettina Knapp, in her excellent work *A Jungian Approach to Literature*, describes this phenomenon in relationship to the story of *The Bacchae.*[2]

When Angelo meets Isabella, his house of cards collapses, and he, who has attempted to remain bright and untarnished by his own humanity, suddenly is confronted by the black hole of his own shadow side. Jung tells us that the brighter the persona, the darker the shadow. Thus, Angelo's darkness is attracted not to an ordinary woman but to Isabella, a woman who is known for her own purity. His shadow side must destroy not only his own, but another's virtue as well.

Even more is invested in Angelo's attraction to Isabella. His anima, which he projects onto her, has become contaminated by falseness to himself. He has abandoned Mariana, his true anima, and attempts to possess, in Isabella, a false anima projection of the impossible virtue he is attempting to achieve in himself. When he sees Isabella, he becomes Narcissus, passionately obsessed with the idea of possessing his own image.

What then of poor Claudio, trapped in prison for the most natural and loving acts, sexual union with the woman who is, in the eyes of all but the state and her family, his wife? He is the ego, the natural man, banished by a tyrannical and impossible persona. His preference for substance over form and for love over law makes him an impossible embarrassment to the tyrannical persona. He has been banished, literally, down into the prison of the unconscious, where he awaits extinction for the crime of being human. There is also much merit to the argument that Claudio is, as a sexual being, a shadow figure for the chaste Angelo, and certainly the two views are not mutually exclusive. To be sure, each character can embody the characteristics of more than one archetype.

That Lucio functions as the main shadow figure seems likely, if for his name alone. Clearly, Shakespeare meant for Lucio to represent the fallen angel that Angelo might have been. But this Lucio is also a bringer of light, in that it is he who brings Isabella to Angelo, thus igniting the blaze that eventually brings light out of darkness.

Lucio is Angelo's shadow double in behavior as well. He lies, he postures, he does everything within his power to avoid the plain truth. And, as shadows often contain some of the good qualities which we repress, he also, despite his many faults, possesses a degree of compassion that Angelo's puritan rigor has rejected.

Pompey, along with his retinue of dissolutes, represents the trickster, who in adolescent psyches, young or old, creates of sex a lurid welter of forbidden and unhealthy pleasures. His contemporary equivalent can still be found in every major city in the world, plying his sad trade of trickery to those who, like Angelo, have banished sex to the dark underside of life.

Among the inmates of the prison, or unconscious, are two minor characters who nonetheless occupy important symbolic positions in this drama. The Provost, who at every opportunity attempts to help Claudio, represents, along with the duke, the self, which is constantly working toward individuation and wholeness. Barnardino, characterized in the cast list as "a dissolute prisoner," stands in direct opposition to him as those parts of the unconscious that do all in their power to remain safely comatose within the sheltering walls of the prison of the unconscious. Confrontation between the conscious and unconscious parts of the psyche is always a difficult, painful experience. It is far easier for most of us to remain in our drunken slumbers and, like Barnardino, avoid the pain.

Last we come to Escalus, the wise old man of myth and legend, who, as a sort of counterbalance to the childish trickster, attempts to keep us on the straight and narrow. Like many another of his kind, Escalus speaks into deaf ears, as Angelo presses on, deeper and deeper, into folly and confusion. Escalus meets with better success in his other role, however, which is that of chorus or raisonneur, a sort of compass the audience can use to find the moral north by which the playwright calculates his direction.

The Duke, always a difficult figure, gives no hint of his purpose in the opening scene. For the naive reader or audience member, his commendation of Angelo is unambiguous, but in the topsy-turvy world of moral confusion, we may be sure: "Things aren't always what they seem/Skimmed milk masquerades as cream."[3] A second look reveals the beginning of the self-enlightenment that this play represents.

In the midst of the Duke's extravagant hymn to Angelo's virtue, he slips in his first small hint;

> Heaven doth with us as we with torches do,
> Not light them for themselves, for if our virtues
> Did not go forth of us, 'twere all alike
> As if we had them not. (I.i, 32-35)

What sounds as innocent as the admonition not to hide his light under a bushel might also be read as a warning that those who care more for their own virtues than for the betterment of their fellow man, might just as well not possess those virtues. Angelo has been blinded by his own shining self-righteousness. He needs to descend into his own darkness in order to find the true light of self-enlightenment instead.

Shakespeare allows us to glimpse much more of the Duke's true intent in his meeting with Friar Thomas. As long as we continue to regard him as a ruler who lacks the courage to enforce his own laws, he elicits more contempt than sympathy. But if we change our focus completely, as we do with an optical illusion, we suddenly see an entirely new picture embedded in the original. Yes, it is the picture of a Grecian urn, but blink, and now it is the picture of two profiles facing each other instead.

Surely it is possible to hear the self speaking about an arrested individuation process when he uses the metaphor of the overgrown lion in the cave "that goes not out to prey." Ostensibly, the metaphor refers to laws that have not been enforced, but the image speaks not of law but of nature. For everything there is a season, and Angelo seems to be frozen in the snows of early spring long past the time when the summer sun should have brought the warmth of manhood to his blood.

For the self too it is possible to admit fallibility. In his conversation with the Friar, the Duke is quick to admit his own culpability in not having enforced the laws because of his preference for retirement and seclusion. Like Prospero, he has neglected public duties for the pleasure of private contemplation, and now he sets forth on the quest of bringing the various qualities into harmony and balance.

His last remarks in the scene might be a commentary on his own behavior, although they refer to Angelo: "hence shall we see if power changes purpose" The conventional and easier assumption is that power should not, in fact, change purpose, but looking deeper, we see that sometimes it must, because a life lived for the public good is not the same as one lived solely for personal gratification. Shakespeare's point about the responsibility of power is a recurring theme in much of the canon. It can also be viewed, on a personal level, as the responsibility of the self to bring balance and wholeness to the individual, just as the "Royal Self," should bring balance and wholeness to the state.

Clearly, balance is the missing element in the world of this play. Harold Goddard makes the point that Mistress Overdone might serve as a symbol for her society.[4] Nearly everyone in this play is overdone in one way or another. Angelo and Isabella seem, quite logically at times, to be reacting against a society that might make any sensitive person sick of sex. Lucio's cynicism has grown out of his immersion in that society Angelo has completely eschewed. Thus we see two sides of the same useless coin, two characters whose lives revolve around sex, making it either a god or a devil instead of a healthy part of human experience.

Lucio might well ask Claudio, when he sees him under arrest, "whence comes this restraint?" Restraint is precisely what is needed in order to free this society from another kind of prison, which Claudio describes as

> too much liberty, my Lucio, liberty:
> As surfeit is the father of much fast,
> So every scope by the immoderate use
> Turns to restraint. Our natures do pursue,
> Like rats that ravin down their proper bane
> A thirsty evil; and when we drink we die. (I.ii, 125-30)

Claudio, because of his capacity for objectivity, has become an inconvenience for Angelo. Like all autocrats, Angelo cannot afford dissension, within or without himself. He enforces the statute, that "drowsy and neglected act" not because of his affection for the rule of law but in order to reinforce the legitimacy of his own attitudes. Claudio is, in effect, a political prisoner, a fact that he demonstrates is not lost on him by his remarks to Lucio near the end of the second scene. Whether it is Angelo's own character or merely his impression of what the office demands, Claudio explains, one thing seems certain, "tis surely for a name."

And there is Shakespeare's old question again: what's in a name? Doctor, lawyer, Indian chief, Montague, movie star, politician, salesman, soldier; all serve as names for the personas we adopt in order to function in the world, our necessary social and professional identities. But underneath the mask of the persona lies all the complexity that is the human psyche. For many like Angelo, these complexities become too painful, and they are repressed into the prison of the unconscious, where they silently await their opportunity to escape.

Isabella, as the anima, finds her opportunity when she is summoned to save her brother from sure death. Jung tells us that typically our first archetypal encounter is with the shadow, and that is followed by confrontation with our contra-sexual archetype, the anima or animus. Angelo, who has tried to shield himself from all contact with his humanity, is cleverly ambushed by the shadow in the form of Lucio when he brings Isabella before him as petitioner.

It is necessary to note here that Lucio's shadow role is much in the tradition of the medieval Vice figure. He is banal, trivial, and without doubt, entertaining.[5] He might be regarded as the shadow of Angelo's persona, with no more substance than that which he reflects. His is not evil on the scale of an Iago, because that role is filled by Angelo himself. Having banished all but his persona into the unconscious, Angelo is like an empty carapace. Like Eliot's hollow men, he is ripe for possession by his own shadow in all its terrifying malignity.

At the beginning of their first encounter, Isabella knows exactly whom she is addressing. Clearly, it is at the persona that she aims this barb:

> Well, believe this,
> No ceremony that to great ones 'longs,
> Not the king's crown, nor the deputed sword,
> The marshal's truncheon, nor the judge's robe,

> Become them with one half so good a grace
> As mercy does. (II.ii, 57-63)

This is anima, talk, at its best and highest. The values of love, mercy, kindness, and compassion soften the absolute values of patriarchal thinking. So many of Shakespeare's anima figures, Portia, Juliet, Rosalind, Isabella, all combine the traditionally female quality of eros with a solidly practical logos faculty. Archetypes are not respecters of personas, and Isabella makes that abundantly clear:

> but man, proud man,
> Dress'd in a little brief authority,
> Most ignorant of what he's most assur'd
> His glassy essence, like an angry ape,
> Plays such fantastic tricks before high heaven
> As makes the angels weep; who, with our spleens,
> Would all themselves laugh mortal. (II.ii, 117-22)

Here, surely, is not a humorless puritan, but a woman who is capable of conjuring laughing angels to help her win her point.

Angelo's turn comes suddenly, after she instructs him to look into his own heart before he condemns her brother to certain death. Apparently it takes only the smallest push to make Angelo aware of his feelings. Unfortunately, that push, rather than prompting a compassionate change, merely throws him into the deepest confusion. For the first time he begins to question himself, and his journey toward individuation has begun.

His first step on the path to self-knowledge is battle with the shadow, and it is that battle that involves all of Angelo's efforts until the final scene. His first groping questions about himself ring true, as he asks himself who he is and whether he loves Isabel. Then, ingrained attitudes take over, and he imagines himself as the victim of some particular temptation:

> O cunning enemy, that to catch a saint,
> With saints dost bait thy hook! Most dangerous
> Is that temptation that doth goad us on
> To sin in loving virtue. . . (II.ii, 179-82)

For Angelo, love has lost its meaning, and sex has become synonymous with sin. Isabella's virtue takes on the characteristics of a sexual fetish for him, because for an individual who has repressed all sexual feelings, only the forbidden can call them forth again.

Upon his next entrance, Angelo has progressed from confusion to distraction, in the knowledge of his own shadow side. The icy facade has melted, exposing raw passions, and Angelo recognizes his own humanity as well as his own capacity for evil:

> . . . Blood, thou art blood.
> Let's write "good angel" on the devil's horn,
> 'Tis not the devil's crest. (II.iv, 15-17)

But the beginning of knowledge precedes the beginning of wisdom, usually by a long period of time.

Angelo can accept his sexuality, not as a natural human trait but only as one of a number of "filthy vices":

> . . . It were as good
> To pardon him that hath from nature stol'n
> A man already made, as to remit
> Their saucy sweetness that do coin heaven's image
> In stamps that are forbid. 'Tis all as easy
> Falsely to take away a life true made
> As to put metal in restrained means
> To make a false one. (II.iv, 42-49)

This equation of murder with Claudio's offense is perhaps the play's strongest statement of moral confusion and one that says much to our own time. When violence and annihilation become equally or more acceptable than love and creation, then Mars has become our ruling symbol, and the potential for global self-destruction looms large and solid.

It is Isabella's appealing honesty that finally catapults Angelo straight into his shadow possession. When she remarks, sensibly, "'Tis set down so in heaven, but not in earth," he imagines that she might be available after all, and throwing away all scruples, he determines to use her brother's life as a way of possessing her.

Then, rather amusingly, he becomes somewhat peevish over her naivete. The habit of moral superiority is still with him, despite his change of heart, and he projects his own shadow qualities onto the as yet innocent Isabella. First he accuses her of being disingenuous, proceeds to degrade and objectify her for being a woman, and ends with crude threats of greater pain to Claudio if she will not accede to his demands.

Angelo's shadow possession becomes complete in this scene, when he announces:

> . . . I have begun,
> And now I give my sensual race the rein.
> Fit thy consent to my sharp appetite,
> Lay by all nicety and prolixious blushes
> That banish what they sue for; . . . (II.iv, 159-63)

Now the persona has become, once more, only a mask for the reality underneath. Angelo has begun to know who he is, and the news so far has been all bad. When angels fall, they have a long way to go. Angelo's fall illustrates Jung's claim that the brighter the persona appears, the darker the shadow will be.

Isabella, meanwhile, has begun to come to terms with her own contradictions. It is important here to reiterate the notion that, as our perspective shifts between literal and psychological reality, we need to consider Isabella, not only as an anima figure, but as a character in her own right. She, too, begins the journey toward self-knowledge, as she is faced with the dilemma of reconciling her moral convictions with her actions. When Angelo confronts her with the fact that she has characterized her brother's actions as more "a merriment than a vice," she is sincerely shocked at her own lack of consistency:

> O, pardon me, my lord, it oft falls out,
> To have what we would have, we speak not what we mean.
> I something do excuse the thing I hate,
> For his advantage that I dearly love. (II.iv, 117-21)

Those who accuse Isabella of coldness seem to forget these words. Her confusion about putting her chastity above her brother's life may seem incomprehensible to contemporary readers, but a brief look at the tradition out of which she formed her opinions should put that decision in context. For the Roman Catholic church, virginity represented the highest form of virtue. Only the celibate could aspire to the highest heavenly honors. When a woman took her holy vows, she became, in the eyes of the church, a bride of Christ. A woman like Isabella might conceivably have considered it preferable to lose her life than to lose her virginity. She might also, an imminent novitiate, have regarded that vow already contracted, so that loss of virginity would have meant commission of a mortal sin.[6] Thus her statement that Claudio would lose his mortal life, but her loss would be eternal.

In the third act, the forces of good begin to converge and to work together toward growth. For the first time, the self, in the person of the Friar/Duke, guided by his constant ally, the Provost, meets the imprisoned and deflated ego, Claudio. The merger of ruler and holy man comprises a particularly apt incarnation for the self in Jung's characterization. The self is not only a manifestation of the best in each individual, that ideal of individuation toward which we strive on a personal level. On a transpersonal level, as part of the collective unconscious, the self is also that spark of the divine within each human begin, the God in us, which makes us part of the anima mundi, the world soul.

Seen in that light, the Friar/Duke's behavior takes on a very different character. When he counsels the wretched prisoner to "Be absolute for death," enumerating in detail the many ills and sorrows of the flesh, we see, instead of the rather sadistic prank that it sometimes appears to be, the beginning of initiation into wisdom. Thus Claudio, in all sincerity, finds in the Friar's words the peace of an easy heart. The ego, set free from its constant search for gratification, rests in the peace that the self provides, and the process of merger begins.

Claudio's stay in prison might correspond roughly to the dark night of the soul or, more secularly, to the period of ego alienation just prior to encounter with the self which Edward F. Edinger describes so vividly in his *Ego and Archetype.*[7] Only through such periods of alienation can the soul search continue to prosper. In the prison of the unconscious Claudio undergoes the necessary abasement that permits him to become aware of the frailty of life and of man. Pain and the influence of the self are hard teachers, but it is only through their instruction that the ego can continue its journey toward individuation.

Isabella's visit, on the other hand, might be regarded as one more roadblock on this pilgrimage. While her sisterly concern initially evokes his courageous protests, the dawning realization of her meaning plunges Claudio back into the torture of ambivalence. His anguished litany on the terrors of death provides a very human counterpoint to the Friar's earlier speech about the miseries of life.

> The weariest and most loathed worldly life
> That age, ache, [penury], end imprisonment
> Can lay on nature is a paradise
> To what we fear of death. (III.i, 128-31)

It couldn't be stated more clearly. The ego does not want to die, to be subsumed into the self, even though that might represent a state of bliss beyond our dreams. Life, with all its difficulties, is sweet, and moreover, it is all we know. Claudio begs Isabella to ransom his life, and she reacts with decidedly unsaintlike fury.

> O you beast!
> O faithless coward! O dishonest wretch!
> Wilt thou be made a man out of my vice?
> Is't not a kind of incest, to take life
> From thine own sister's shame? What should I think?
> Heaven shield my mother play'd my father fair
> For such a warped slip of wilderness
> Ne'er issu'd from his blood. Take my defiance!
> Die, perish! Might but my bending down
> Reprieve thee from thy fate, it should proceed.
> I'll pray a thousand prayers for thy death,
> No word to save thee. (III.i, 135-46)

How do we account for this sudden vicious turn in a woman renowned for her gentleness and virtue? The source of Isabella's lasting intrigue is her complexity. Like Angelo, she has fallen in love with her own saintly persona. She has crafted a masterpiece, as did Pygmalion, and has begun to worship her own graven image. Claudio's very human response to her attitude calls all her attitudes into question, and she fights like a cornered animal to avoid that discomfort.

Isabella, as anima figure, works within the overall scheme of the play, but here we see Isabella the woman, coming to terms with her own animus. The positive side of that animus has revealed itself in the strong, logical argument with which she captured Angelo's attention. Now, pushed to her limits, she exhibits its negative side.

Jung says that the animus, unlike the anima, is not likely to manifest itself in an erotic mood; rather, it is more likely to

> take the form of a hidden "sacred" conviction. When such a conviction is preached with a loud, insistent masculine voice or imposed on others by means of brutal emotional scenes, the underlying masculinity in a woman is easily recognized. However, even in a woman who is outwardly very feminine the animus can be an equally hard, inexorable power. One may suddenly find oneself up against something in a woman that is obstinate, cold, and completely inaccessible."[8]

This may well be poor Claudio's first encounter with the animus at its worst, and he quite understandably exits the scene with the remark that he is sufficiently out of love with life to be well rid of it. Clearly, his relations with Juliet have been of a different order. Her brief appearance in the second act reveals a mature and compassionate attitude toward both sexes as part of the same whole, the model for an integrated animus, just as Claudio serves as the model for an integrated anima. When the Duke/Friar asks if she loves the man who wronged her, she replies, "Yes, as I love the woman that wrong'd him." Further probing by the Friar shows her willing to repent if necessary, but clearly she is convinced that theirs was an act of mutual love and deserves no punishment in a just world.

Jung was capable, it should be noted, of becoming quite rabid himself on the subject of the animus rampant. In "Aion: Phenomenology of the Self" he claims that "no man can converse with an animus for five minutes without becoming the victim of his own anima." He declares further "Often the man has the feeling--*and he is not altogether wrong*--that only seduction or a beating or rape would have the necessary power of persuasion."[9]

In order to maintain objectivity in the face of such a statement, it is necessary to remind ourselves that Jung was a product of the phallocentric, repressive, conservative European society in which he lived. Moreover, the malice with which he describes the animus in this section might quite literally be the greatest argument for his theory. Such shocking invective must surely come straight from his own enraged anima, as he suggests, wittingly or unwittingly, in the same section, "Men can argue in a very womanish way, too, when they are anima-possessed and have thus been transformed into the animus of their own anima."

This looking glass of Jung's shows us a world that certainly does get "curiouser and curiouser." But certainly most curious of all is that much of what we see looks remarkably, sometimes embarrassingly familiar.

In dealing with the societal, sexist bias of Jung's theories, however, it is necessary to consider the question of mutability in the archetypes. Are they set in their Procrustean bed for all times, all places, all peoples, with no possibility of change? Literature, as the best history of the collective psyche that we possess, seems to answer that question far better than psychology, which is, comparatively speaking, still in its infancy.

Part of the confusion here, it might be argued, stems from Jung's own lack of precise terminology. He often interchanges the terms archetype and archetypal image, causing much confusion as to how culture-specific these forces are. Post-Jungians, however, seem to be fairly clear in their consensus that the archetype itself, as a structural unit of the unconscious, is merely an expectation or a tendency toward certain behavior in oneself and others. Thus societies can change radically, but our unconscious, having no sense of time or place, is able to adapt to any situation. Like a troupe of brilliantly innovative actors, our archetypes fit themselves into whatever parts are available to them in each individuation drama, but they always maintain, under the mask of the actor, the archetypal characteristics that are common to all mankind.

Moreover, it is necessary to remember that, admittedly, Jung's description of the anima is in large part garnered from inner experience, while his animus descriptions were secondhand at best. He remarks in a number of the works that while the anima experience seems clear to men, the women with whom he worked often had difficulty in recognizing the animus within them. His view of the animus was formed more by what he observed than by what women described about their own animus feelings.

This might be regarded as an example of culturally influenced archetypal experience, in that men of Jung's generation felt more freedom in examining their sexual impulses than did women. The anima, as a recognizable archetypal symbol for man, was quite acceptable in the context of both virgin and whore, whichever the occasion demanded. The animus, on the other hand, had to rely on disguise in order to be compatible with the nineteenth century's notion of what a woman should want.

The question of what a woman wants, which eluded Dr. Freud so completely, might have been made clear to him had he taken the time to read some nineteenth-century women writers. The Bronte sisters, notably, made use of the animus figure in their work, immortalizing in Heatchcliff and Rochester the Byronic figure of sexual potency and latent danger which spoke so powerfully to women who felt such utter lack of those qualities.[10] Isabella speaks for all women in her first encounter with Angelo, as her animus begins to feel the first strong stirrings of life.

> I would to heaven I had your potency,
> And you were Isabel! Should it then be thus?
> No; I would tell what 'twere to be a judge,
> And what a prisoner. (II.ii, 67-71)

Poor Isabel is as battered by her archetypes as is Angelo by his. His meeting with her comprises an overwhelming encounter with the anima that he had successfully repressed for so many years, and with it his sexuality and his eros function "even like an o'ergrown lion in a cave." His inability to accept his own human feelings of sexual desire and love forces them into the dark, seamy shadow realm that his society has shown him is their natural locale.

Isabel, also a prisoner of her persona, is thrown into a similar confusion by a dark, powerful, violent animus, a part of her own psyche completely unfamiliar to her. Jung describes the anima and animus encounter as creating much the same effect, which amounts to a feeling of "unshakable rightness and righteousness."[11] He goes on to describe the totally irrational moods that often follow such an event,

> Consciousness is fascinated by it, held captive, as if hypnotized. Very often the ego experiences a vague feeling of moral defeat and then behaves all the more defensively, defiantly, and self-righteously, thus setting up a vicious circle which only increases its feeling of inferiority. The bottom is then knocked out of the

> human relationship, for like megalomania a feeling of inferiority makes mutual recognition impossible, and without this there is no relationship.[12]

Fortunately for Isabel, the self is on the job, and having heard all between her and Claudio, proceeds to instruct her, not with angry blame but with love, as a wise parent who appeals to the best in a wayward child. Praising her beauty and goodness, the Friar/Duke forbears to mention her cruel outburst at Claudio. Instead, he uses kindly guile in pretending he has no doubt she will find a way to "content this substitute and save your brother."

The word substitute works nicely here as a description of Angelo. First as persona, now as shadow, he furnishes a sorry substitute for the integrated personality that the self continues to seek. In this context, Isabella's own characterization of Angelo as an "outward sainted devil" contains an ironic core, in view of her own behavior after her first animus encounter. The "outward sainted" personas behind which both Isabel and Angelo attempt to hide are only whited sepulchres, covering the pharisaical devils that dwell within the human soul.

The Duke/Friar's bed trick, coupled with his Machiavellian apology, poses one of this play's most troubling aspects for the contemporary audience, though it may have been less so to an age more accustomed to the idea as a conventional plot device. In Anne Barton's *Riverside* preface, she makes the point that it is not only a sin in the eyes of the church, but represents a union "considerably more dubious" than that of Claudio and Juliet.

Here we must take a Kierkegaardian leap and examine the proposal that the self, the spark of divinity within each individual, does indeed work in mysterious ways. Some of those ways seem to involve the intervention of that most ambiguous of all Jung's archetypes, the trickster. Jung's trickster has a quicksilver quality that defies coherent classification. Like Harlequin, one of his most familiar avatars, he seems to possess multiple personalities.

The trickster makes his appearance frequently in folktale as a vestige of the primitive psyche and a manifestation of the collective, as opposed to the personal, shadow. Anti-intellectual, mischievous, cunning, he crops out in Carnival, in the Festival of Fools, and on Halloween in guises that range from the childlike to the sinister. Tracing the development of this character further, Jung connects him to the shaman, or wounded healer, from which incarnation he eventually moves toward a savior figure. This chain of relativity brings him finally back to a clear correspondence with the self, in Jungian terms, because not only does Jung speak of the self as the divine within us, but he refers to Christ as a symbol for the self. In the following chapters the multiple roles of the trickster will be examined in greater detail as the central motif of each play. In *Measure for Measure,* despite its atmosphere of chicanery and disguise, the trickster is less central to the action. The Friar/Duke, as self, uses the mask of the trickster to bring about the individuation process, both in the case of the bed trick and, later, in what appears to be a cruel cat-and-mouse game with Isabella in regard to her brother's life.

Pride goeth before a fall for Angelo, like all men, because the trickster waits right around the corner, banana peel at the ready. Without the help of the trickster the self would have a much more difficult time maintaining some semblance of psychological balance. Angelo, in the grip of his shadow, is in a dangerous state of inflation, just ripe for a fall.

Archetypes, as autonomous complexes, have a wide range of behavior and quality, depending upon the environment, people, and events that activate them. All, with the exception of the self, appear as incarnations of both good and evil. As an example of that principle in its most extreme form, the shadow of an evil person might be the repository of most of his good qualities. Fairy tales and folktales abound with stories of the good and bad mother and father.

Where on that scale do the denizens of Vienna's demimonde fall? The pimps, the prostitutes, the drunks, and the wastrels of the subplot seem to function largely as a parodic reflection of the main plot. "O heavens, what stuff is here?" cries the Duke, as he surveys the ragtag caricature of society at its lowest ebb.

Here Pompey, as the trickster in his most irresponsible role, uses his wit to trivialize and confuse ethical issues. Lamenting the newly enforced strictures on prostitution, he compares money lenders unfavorably with whores, whose "usury" he categorizes as "merrier." The Duke, disgusted by his first contact with some of his seamiest subjects, sends Pompey off to jail. Thus, the self, attempting to bring order out of chaos, tries to cleanse the personality of some of its less desirable traits.

Lucio carries more than his share of those. His first appearance, in the second scene, introduces him as a playboy whose ideas of humor seem to revolve entirely around venereal diseases. The difference between him and Pompey is that Pompey is content with a more or less professional attention to the business of pimping. Lucio, on the other hand, goes much farther in carrying out his shadow duties. He is a pathological liar who, most significantly, lies to and about the self.

Lucio's greatest sin is the opposite of Angelo's, who as a self-righteous hypocrite, condemns sexuality, along with other human traits. Conversely, Lucio trivializes sexuality along with other human traits. They represent two extremes in the badly unbalanced universe of this play. While Angelo denies the body, Lucio denies the soul.

Destructiveness is Lucio's ruling characteristic. In his nihilism, he attempts to destroy reputations in order to bring everyone else down to his level. Despising himself and everyone else, he takes nothing seriously, again in direct opposition to Angelo, who displays a puritanical disdain for humor of all kinds.

The self, on the other hand, in the Duke shows a rather ironic sense of humor which manifests itself in various ways. While Lucio, like an obnoxious stand-up comedian, uses humor as a cover for his vitriolic gossip, the Friar/Duke remarks with dry sarcasm, "You are pleasant, Sir, and speak apace." The irony is completely lost on Lucio, who lacks real humor, which must incorporate the ability to see our own foibles as well as those of others.

We are what we eat, in the body, and just as surely our intellectual and spiritual growth is determined by what we think. What a society or an individual finds laughable is one of the most telling indicators of mental, moral, and, often, of physical condition, as well. The English director Peter Brook dramatized this point tellingly some years ago in a play called *The Ik.*[13] The title refers to a primitive tribe that managed, with difficulty, to live a marginal life, constantly on the brink of starvation. For these people, the subject of off-color humor was not sex but food. In totalitarian countries, we are told, political jokes get the biggest laughs. For students raised in strict parochial schools, nun jokes are frequently the funniest.[14]

The Vienna of this play is diseased, physically and spiritually. Sexuality has been perverted from a natural human function to a subject of childish, twisted humor or unnatural horror. The value system of this city has become dysfunctional, so that people either overvalue or undervalue sex as a whole. Angelo and Isabella's conduct is, in a sense, an overvaluation in that it removes sexuality from the normal range of human behavior and creates a false idol out of celibacy. Lucio's society, on the other hand, degrades the whole area and turns it into nothing but a dirty joke.

In humor, of course, we always feel the presence of the trickster. True to his schizophrenic character, he can appear in any number of forms. In constructive form his childish sense of play can rescue us from despair, while his less benign forms can cause mayhem and destruction. Clearly, the trickster plays some part in the behavior of the Friar/Duke, and those aspects of his conduct prove difficult to accept until it is possible to see his actions as providing a necessarily rocky path to salvation.

His deceit of Isabella in the matter of her brother's death is the most outstanding example of ostensibly cruel trickster behavior. But Isabella suffers from the sins of pride and self-righteousness. Her final ability to set aside her own outrage and intercede on behalf of Mariana is an act of grace that finally cleanses Isabella. Both as woman and as anima figure, she needs to integrate the compassion and selflessness that are sorely missing in the cold and "holy" virgin. That final act of forgiveness, of divine grace, is really the crux of the play's action. Like the Countess in *The Marriage of Figaro,* whose final aria is a miracle of grace, Isabella's act should touch the heart of every audience member or reader.

Returning once more to Peter Brook, in his ground-breaking commentary on the contemporary theatre *The Empty Space,* he writes:

> If we follow the movement in *Measure for Measure* between the Rough and the Holy we will discover a play about justice, mercy, honesty, forgiveness, virtue, virginity, sex and death: kaleidoscopically one section of the play mirrors the other, it is in accepting the prism as a whole that its meanings emerge. When I once staged the play I asked Isabella, before kneeling for Angelo's life, to pause each night until she felt the audience could take it not longer-and this used to lead to a two-minute stopping of the play. The device became a voodoo pole - a silence in which all the invisible elements of the evening came together, a silence in which the abstract motion of mercy became concrete for that moment to those present.[15]

Brook's notion of what he categorizes as the "Rough and the Holy" theatre certainly merge in this, one of Shakespeare's most peculiar masterpieces. Considering Jung's characterization of Christ as a symbol of the self brings the Friar/Duke's actions into much clearer focus. The self pushes, prods, and leads us toward the best of which we are capable. Often, when we are most intractable, the self must seek the benign help of the trickster in order to get the job done.

In considering the duality of the archetypes at work within the Duke, it becomes apparent that the actor playing that part can influence our perceptions of which archetype is dominant within any one character. If the trickster is dominant, the play loses its focus, but if the trickster is entirely absent, the character becomes incomprehensible. Therefore the part must be played with wisdom, with gentle, never capricious humor, in order to remain psychologically comfortable. A recent American production lost its impact because the Duke, played by a seasoned actor, seemed more a mischievous child than a wise parent.[16] Clearly, a director might choose to portray the part that way, but such a decision will result in a very different play than one in which we feel the presence of the self working toward proper individuation.

Pompey, of course, furnishes an image of the trickster at his most irresponsible and inappropriate. We meet him, early in the play, making broad, generally unpleasant jokes about sexuality. Now, in Act IV, he demonstrates his inability to find substance in any thing. He jokes about death as blithely as he does about sex, combining the two with clumsy wit when he discusses his fitness for the job of executioner, declaring that he can cut off the head of a bachelor but never a married man, because he can never cut off a woman's head, referring both to head of household and to maidenhead.

In contrast, the Provost, as an agent of the self, remains a fixed point of reason in this welter of moral confusion. When Abhorson, the executioner, expresses concern about his profession's being brought down by the addition of a bawd, the Provost dryly remarks, "Go to, sir, you weigh equally; a feather will turn the scale" (IV.ii, 30-31).

The ability to recognize truth and falsehood, regardless of the guises in which they appear, is a mark of the self. The Provost can make those determinations, but Angelo, in his confusion, is capable of making the most disastrous mistakes. The whole plot revolves around the incredible fact that Angelo can equate an act of love between two people who are pledged to each other with an act of prostitution. He, as a hollow persona, relies wholly on received opinions, rather than on thoughtful, personal decisions.

In contrast to all the active participants in this drama, we come now to Barnardino, who spends most of the play (and apparently his life) in a drunken stupor:

> A man that apprehends death no more dreadfully but
> as a drunken sleep, careless, reckless, and fearless of
> what's past, present, or to come; insensible
> of mortality, and desperately mortal. (IV.ii, 142-45)

"What a piece of work is man!" Barnardino is Everyman, to some extent certainly; the only animal, so far as we know, who is aware of his own mortality and who spends most of his life trying desperately to remain insensible to it. Harold Goddard considers him to be the play's most intriguing character: "Like Falstaff. . . [he] tempts the imagination to play around him."[17] And so indeed he does. What engaged audience member has not wondered where he comes from and where he goes. Living consciously is much more difficult and painful than remaining unconscious and blundering through. No doubt that is why so much of humanity chooses that method, but Shakespeare gives us Barnardino as a model of escape from oblivion. It is only after he is freed that the final integration and reconciliation can take place.

Isabella learns, to her sorrow, that life allows no spectators, only participants and those who, like Barnardino, choose not to live at all. Her entrance in the third Scene of Act IV reveals a woman greatly changed from the girlish imitation of virtue in earlier scenes. Gone too is the self-righteousness of that girl, as the woman cries: "Unhappy Claudio! Wretched Isabel! Injurious world! Most damned Angelo!" (IV.iii, 121-22)

She has learned one of life's most painful lessons: sometimes our very best efforts are to no avail. The world is, indeed, an injurious place, and the good do not always triumph.

It is in this scene too that Lucio reveals some of his good shadow qualities. Unlike the cold, fanatical Angelo, Lucio is capable of both compassion and affection. His speech to Isabel rings true when he laments her red eyes and declares that he loved her brother. His is certainly the charm of the scoundrel, the appeal of the vice figure in its more innocuous form. Even the Duke admits it when he says, "Sir, your company is fairer than honest," as he exits the scene, reluctantly suffering Lucio's persistent company.

Like a mirror image of the departing pair, Angelo and Escalus appear next on the scene. Angelo, now darker by far, has become his own shadow, making Lucio's modest attempts at vice appear quite paltry, making of him a sort of parody of evil, that part which we all too often confuse for the real thing. Escalus, as the wise old man, parallels the Duke himself, as one of his agents. On one side good dwarfs evil; on the other evil overshadows good.

Nonetheless, it is here that the scales start to tip irrevocably toward a climax in which the angels carry the day. In his soliloquy, Angelo, quite literally, begins to "come to himself" after a period of possession by other parts of the psyche. He repents his actions, the supposed rape of Isabella, and the intended murder of Claudio, finally crying out in despair: "Alack, when once our grace we have forgot,/ Nothing goes right; we would, and we would not" (IV.iv, 33-34). So, the forces gather for the final battle, in full knowledge of where they stand. Angelo, still attempting to preserve the facade he has built, is prepared to lie outright to the Duke, to be, quite consciously, as false as he had been unconsciously before the Duke disappeared. He has gone as far down as he can go in terms of conscious and intentional evil, and he is, imperceptively, beginning the long climb back because repentance is the first step toward salvation.

Act V's long, convoluted scene has about it the feel of a fairy-tale, in much the same way that *All's Well* does. The Friar/Duke now assumes the character of a puppeteer, as he manipulates his marionettes from above and produces miracle upon miracle for their general confusion. Isabella, like the heroine of folktale, must complete the tasks assigned to her before she receives her reward.

As the chief anima figure in this drama, Isabel, like the other characters, requires close attention here. Viewed as an actual woman, she excites admiration and pity as she moves through the Duke's maze to discover the truth at the end. She has grown into a strong, independent thinker, a woman to be reckoned with, and one whose final defense of Angelo raises her even further in the estimation of the observer. How then can we reconcile ourselves to the Duke's assumption that she is willing and able to leave her chosen calling and meekly agree to be his wife?

The answer, of course, is that we cannot, not even by the standards of Shakespeare's own time. His heroines do not simply wait to be chosen. They often do the choosing themselves, within the confines of the society in which they operate and, more importantly, within the context of the play itself.

But moving our prism just a little and seeing her once more as an anima figure, an autonomous complex, the whole scene falls into place with graceful ease. Angelo's anima, like most of his personality, was nonoperational at the play's point of attack. Surveying its several parts, we can understand why so much work was needed. Isabel, as the chief anima figure, was shut up in a convent, away from the dangers of the worldly, sexual life. Mariana was exiled and disgraced by false accusations, also of a sexual nature. Juliet, the natural woman, pregnant and unashamed, was deprived of her husband. The fates of these three demonstrate Angelo's horror not only of sex but of the feminine itself, of his own anima. Only Mistress Overdone, a lurid parody of the anima in the virgin/whore model, remains free, by living an outlaw life and just managing to stay ahead of the authorities.

Because Angelo, as shadow/persona, is incapable of healing his own illness, it remains for the self to initiate the process of individuation. Just as the self has forced the anima to be strong and to seek justice, he then brings her to him as a vital part of the whole. Their union transcends the ordinary and encompasses, in its symbolism, the whole of the individuation process. In Jungian terms, they represent the alchemical marriage of the king and queen, the mystical *coniunctio.* The Duke, a secular prince, also incorporates the sacred in his role of Friar. Isabella, in becoming his mate, is not only queen, on a symbolic level, but also the Holy Virgin, a mother figure, so that the symbolism becomes complete. They have decontaminated the male/female union for Angelo by becoming that androgynous alchemical whole of man/woman, mother/father, king/queen.

All this occurs at the moment that Claudio, the banished ego, is released from the prison of the unconscious, to the great relief of Angelo, who learns that he has not murdered that part of himself after all. The dreadful destruction inspired by his imbalance is not, after all, real, but merely, as Isabel explains,

> For Angelo,
> His act did not o'ertake his bad intent,

> And must be buried but as an intent
> That perish'd by the way. Thoughts are no subjects;
> Intents, but merely thoughts. (V.i, 450-54)

It might all have been Angelo's bad dream, this Viennese misadventure that finally comes right. And what are dreams, in the Jungian sense, but expressions of the unconscious speaking to us in our sleep, attempting to guide us toward finding ourselves?

Pompey, Overdone, and their rather pathetic, tattered band have faded from sight by this time, like the trickster illusions they are. They represent only a twisted caricature of what life can be, but a true picture of what life becomes for those who do not find its center in the self. The trickster comes and goes, according to the situation in which the psyche finds itself. For one who has progressed far enough along the road to individuation, perhaps his chores are reduced to the pleasant duties of providing the ability to laugh at oneself and with others. Certainly, those among us who have chosen the path of spiritual growth as their main life's work seem far from gloomy. As cases in point, the Dalai Lama, Mother Theresa, and Gandhi all seem to have found laughter easy.

The ego, the persona, the anima, the trickster, and the self are present and accounted for, but what about the shadow? Returning for a moment to the beginning of the act, his behavior is clearly a burlesque echo of Angelo's. Lucio's malign shadow qualities shrink in inverse proportion as Angelo reaches the zenith of *his* shadow behavior. Angelo lies coolly, convincingly, attempting to discredit Isabella. Angelo has finally become so thoroughly corrupt that his shadow is, indeed, becoming his better part. As the scene progresses, Angelo maintains his posture of evil, denying Mariana coldly, while Lucio leaps from side to side, trying to hold together the fabric of his lies about the Duke and the Friar. Lucio, the shadow, becomes merely a parody of evil, while Angelo, "most damned Angelo," grows into the very type of evil itself.

On a microcosmic level, Lucio's final fate serves as a reminder of Angelo's final salvation. Angelo, as he makes his honest confession, craving death for his sins, has finally integrated his shadow. He has recognized the evil within himself and has claimed full responsibility for it. Then, as the self aids him in integration of the anima, Lucio is united with the shadow of that anima, the "punk," an image of the completely devalued feminine. The shadow, having joined the ranks of the unemployed, disappears from the scene.

The last image of this fairy-tale ending is of the Duke, gathering the remainder of his allies together: the Provost, as an element of the self, and Escalus, the wise old man. A reader might legitimately question the presence of Escalus in this Jungian scheme, in view of the fact that his warnings are all to no avail. The point is, that he is there, speaking truth to Angelo, who, in his confusion and willfulness, refuses to listen.

As for Barnardine, the sleeper awakened, perhaps he is, as Goddard suggests, the most intriguing character of all. Will he, this ". . . stubborn soul/That apprehends no further that this world,/and squar'st [his] life accordingly . . ." really see the drama within and around him and, as the Duke/self suggests, ". . . Pray thee take this mercy to provide/For better times to come" (V.i, 484-85).

Chapter III

I'll Never Grow Up: The Lost Boys in *Troilus and Cressida*

What's aught but as 'tis valued?
(II.ii, 53)

In contrast to the other three plays under consideration, *Troilus and Cressida* is not an individuation drama. Like *Measure for Measure* and *Hamlet*, it deals with a social malaise, but unlike them, it lacks a central focus. Anne Barton pinpoints the situation in her *Riverside* introduction, noting, "The fact that no one character or group of characters in *Troilus and Cressida* can be regarded as being either morally or structurally central is one of the problems of the play."[1]

What we see, instead, is an entire society that has failed to progress toward maturity because it is mired in an early stage of the individuation journey. A society, like an individual, can be possessed by one archetype. Jung refers to Nazi Germany's possession by "the blonde beast," Wotan, who slumbers deep in the German psyche.[2] Bettina Knapp discusses a similar case of possession by the hero archetype in her discussion of Corneille's *Horace.*[3]

The society ruled by this archetype cannot progress to the next stage of its journey, toward maturity and selfhood. Mesmerized by the idea of the quest of honor and glory, bloodshed and victory, such a society continues to replay, over and over, the myth of the hero. This drama, psychologically speaking, symbolizes the young man's journey into independence from the parents, his slaying of the dragon of dependence, and his emergence into manhood and sexuality as he frees the beautiful princess and takes her to wife.

For Troy, however, the quest has become fatally perverted by the abduction of Helen. Paris, as the representative of the society, has won not the virgin princess but the wife of another man. Like Red Cross Knight, he has been duped by his own sensuality. It is Duessa, not Una, these knights strive to protect. The fair princess is not, as is fitting, an object of love but merely one of lust. So this dark, unseemly parody of the hero's quest becomes frozen in time, as two warring armies create an exceedingly poor imitation of heroic behavior.

But what of Helen, the fabled beauty who caused all this chaos? Both Shakespeare and Marlowe before him make a point of revealing her to be nothing more than an ordinary woman, perhaps no more than a rather silly, pretty flirt. That, of course, is the very crux of the matter in anima projection. No one, not Paris nor any member of the Trojan or Greek forces ever really sees Helen. She is not a human being but merely an object upon which this male society can project its unintegrated anima.

Referring to Jung's personality types, we see a society so badly unbalanced that its inferior functions are, for all practical purposes, nonexistent. Completely lacking in reflectivity, these people are extraverted to a fault. Thus their attention is riveted on the exterior object, in this case Helen. They have, as a group, not passed the infantile stage in which the object is internalized, so that they are unable to find any value within themselves, but only in the external world of objects.

So, extraverted as they are and slaves to their own senses, they totally lack the intuitive function. Only occasionally do we see any evidence of intuitive skill among the warriors. In Ulysses, the wily Odysseus, we see an awareness of human nature and an instinct for using that knowledge. Unfortunately he uses it shortsightedly, in an effort to gain immediate ends, rather than to see larger patterns of behavior. In Hector, too, the intuitive impulse is smothered by the pressures of the hero mentality.

As for Jung's rational functions, it seems clear that only a society in which feeling completely overwhelms thinking could such a disastrous situation as the Trojan War ever have come about. What is the psychological reason for a society that has become so fatally unbalanced? One answer might be that no society can be healthy and whole when either its masculine or its feminine component is missing.

Both the Trojans and the Greeks have banished the feminine from their worlds. Helen and her double, Cressida, are never women, but merely objects of male desire, Cressida is no more real to Troilus than Helen is to Paris. They are merely objects upon which male fantasies can be projected. Andromache, who appears as a real woman, not as a male projection, is scorned by Hector when she attempts to warn him about her correct intuition. But most telling of all is Cassandra, whose mad wails are reminiscent of William Blake's haunting portrait of Milton's six-fold emanation, crying for recognition and in a Jungian sense, for integration. Cassandra, in fact, serves as an avatar of intuition, which more than any other quality has been banished from the universe of this play by overvaluation of the sexual object, leading to deification of sensual excess. Poor, foolish Helen, like all man-made sex goddesses before and after her, unwittingly becomes, a *vagina dentata* woman, that fearsome creature from myth and fairy-tale that draws men back into the womb they have sought to escape. She is paradoxically, the antithesis of the feminine. Neither maiden, nor mother, nor crone, she becomes the Terrible Mother disguised, who holds these men in thrall because they will not progress past psychological adolescence. From *puer* to *senex*, in the painfully foolish figure of Nestor, they are subsumed once more into the womb in a sort of Oedipal regression because Helen, as the wife of another man, represents an unlawful or incestuous relationship.

Both traditional qualities of female eros and male logos are perverted in this society, so that the worst traits of both men and women emerge from the chaos. Lacking logos, or logic, the men are possessed by the search for power, violence, and lust. Lacking eros, or relatedness, the women become sensuous, vain, and manipulative. Thersites is the voice of a vile society, rotten clear to its core. Paradoxically, the object of his most vicious excoriation is the one relationship in the play that appears to be based on something like sincere affection, the friendship between Achilles and Patroclus. The integrity of this arguably homosexual bond stands in direct contrast to any other relationship in the play. In this patriarchal world only masculine attachments exist.

The opening scene places us squarely in the familiar world of the courtly lover. The youthful Troilus pours out his self-conscious agonies of love to Pandarus, whom he rebukes for telling him more of Cressida's supposed beauties. The parallels between Cressida and Helen are established immediately, as Pandarus compares their various qualities, affecting pique over the prevalent notion that Helen is more fair than his niece Cressida.

Thus Shakespeare begins by calling into question the whole premise of Helen's fabled beauty, simultaneously illustrating the effect that the society's myth has wrought on this impressionable young man. Troilus's brother Paris has become the embodiment of the hero because he has claimed the prize over which two armies have been fighting for seven long years. Troilus has grown into young manhood with this example constantly before him, the false princess, sequestered within the walled city, embedded like a grain of sand that has grown not into a pearl but into an abscess which infects the entire society.

Pandarus, wise in the ways of the flesh, whets the young man's appetite by creating a false sense of the quest, implying that Cressida is invulnerable to all suits and that Troilus's efforts are in vain. Although he acts as go-between, he never suggests marriage as the proper end of courtship, but merely sexual consummation. That puzzling attitude in people of some obvious social status would appear to be a reflection of the society's central situation, which presents sex as an end in itself and not as a part of the marriage bond. The play's only reference to marriage between the two is in Troilus's "I take today a wife" speech in the second act, and that, given the ensuing events, appears to be more a euphemism than a statement of intent. Thus Troilus's whole posture of courtly love, which revolves around the idea of an unavailable love object, a married woman, becomes a parody of self-delusion and imposture.

Pandarus's parting volley is a criticism of Cressida's refusal to accompany her father into the Greek camp. He expresses exasperation and implies that he has no interest in such a foolish girl.

Here, then, we are faced with the puzzle of Cressida's nature. Why has her priestly father abandoned her to the care of her lascivious uncle? Why has she chosen to stay in Troy if it was indeed a choice, as Pandarus implies? Here is that commonest of Shakespearean heroines, the motherless girl who must find her models of womanhood where she will. Cressida seems to dwell in an all-male world, abandoned, at least temporarily, by her father, and supervised, if we can use that word, by an avuncular pimp. Also tainted by her corrupt world, she appears to be a young woman who has learned to take care of herself out of necessity. She reminds us of nothing so much as a precocious child who has learned to cope in an adult world where the only value is expediency.

Like a starlet whose role model is the reigning Hollywood sex goddess, she has groomed herself for the only job that appears available to a young woman, that of glamorous mistress. Her assets are physical beauty and a ready wit which displays a healthy skepticism about nearly everything except Troilus himself. Her verbal skirmishes with Pandarus bespeak a long acquaintance with his character. Unlike Troilus, she is not naive about Pandarus's aims. Her wit is dry and to the point, as she suffers through one of her uncle's long-winded stories about Helen's flirtation with Troilus concerning a white hair on his chin.

When he finally delivers his punch line, glorifying Troilus's witty innuendo about cuckoldry, and declares, "But there was such laughing! and Helen so blush'd and Paris so chaf'd, and all the rest so laugh'd, that it pass'd," she remarks succinctly "So let it now; for it has been a great while going by" (I.ii, 168-69).

Cressida is no one's fool, except perhaps love's. Clearly, her attraction to Troilus is as strong as his to her. She protects herself as best she can with the only weapons she possesses--words, the sword and buckler of the Elizabethans, that most powerful bulwark against any enemy who threatens the heart's secrets. Pandarus seems genuinely unaware of her feelings for Troilus, marveling at her skill at dissembling when he declares her such a woman that a man knows not at what ward she lies. She declares her distrust toward all the world when she says, with ostensible playfulness but ultimate truth:

> Upon my back, to defend my belly, upon my wit, to defend my wiles, upon my secrecy, to defend mine honesty, my mask, to defend my beauty, and you, to defend all these; and at all these wards I lie, at a thousand watches. (I.ii, 260-64)

When Pandarus counters with, "Say one of your watches," she continues:

> Nay, I'll watch you for that; and that's one
> of the chiefest of them too. If I cannot ward what
> I would not have hit, I Can watch you for telling how
> I took the blow--unless it swell past hiding, and then

it's past watching. (I.ii, 266-70)

There, then, is Cressida's manifesto. This is war for her too, the guerrilla war of the underclass against the power structure, in this case, the patriarchy. She can survive only so long as she keeps her guard up. She can trust no one, least of all her uncle. Her battleground is the sexual arena, and the ultimately telling (swelling) blow is pregnancy for a woman.

The scene's closing monologue makes her position even clearer. She cannot trust even Troilus, whom she loves, because "men prize the thing ungain'd more than it is." And finally: "Then though my heart's content firm love doth bear,/Nothing of that shall from mine eyes appear" (I.ii, 294-95). Why, then, does she acquiesce when Pandarus finally brings her together with Troilus in the third act? It seems clear that her motivation is simple desire. She loves him and finally can no longer bear to keep it from him.

It is for good reason that this play has been compared to *Romeo and Juliet*. Feuding families set up no greater barricades to normal young love than does a society that so corrupts its purpose as this. Juliet's rhapsodies are no more moving than Cressida's when she finally drops the mask of sophisticated caution and confesses to Troilus that she has loved him "night and day for many weary months." She goes on about her fear that he will take advantage of her, once he knows the truth:

If I confess much, you will play the tyrant.
I love you now, but till now not so much
But I might master it. In faith I lie,
My thoughts were like unbridled children grown
Too headstrong for their mother. See, we fools!
Why have I blabb'd? Who shall be true to us,
when we are so unsecret to ourselves?
but though I lov'd you well, I woo'd you not,
And yet, good faith, I wish'd myself a man,
or that we women had men's privilege
Of speaking first. Sweet, bid me hold my tongue,
for in this rapture I shall surely speak
The thing I shall repent. See, see your silence,
[Cunning] in dumbness, from my weakness draws

My very soul of counsel! Stop my mouth. (III.ii, 119-34)

When Troilus does the obvious and kisses her, Pandarus calls the scene, "Pretty, i'faith," clearly believing Cressida's outburst to be part of her artful strategy. Knowing the play's outcome, it is a painfully pathetic moment when she protests in confusion that her remarks were innocent and not intended to be seductive.

The sensitive reader feels real sadness for this girl in no-woman's-land when she mourns the control she sacrificed for love while declaring, in her passion, that it is only "a kind of self," not her true self, that she can entrust to Troilus "to be another's fool." She ends the speech with the telling line "I know not whereof I speak." It is Cressida's unconscious that speaks for her here, warning her that her true self may never be entrusted to another and, most painfully, not to this young man for whom she feels so much love but no real trust.

Cressida's intuitive function works as a proper balance to her sensual side. Likewise, her thinking and feeling modes keep her from going too far in either direction, and her extraversion, as evidenced in her exceptional social skills, is tempered effectively by her capacity for reflective thinking or introversion. She emerges, in fact, despite the miserable role in which fate has cast her, as the most fully human character in the play, with the greatest capacity for mature psychological growth.

In her essay "This Is and Is Not Cressid,"[4] Janet Adelman notes that, as we seem to have established a "privileged relationship" with Cressida at the end of her first scene, we lose that relationship, just as Troilus does, when she betrays him with Diomedes. We see her, then, only through his eyes and never again have direct contact with her as an individual. That, as Adelman rightly points out, is one of the play's most unsettling aspects, one that poses a great problem for the reader, the director, and the actress.

Notwithstanding all those difficulties, it seems logical to assume that Cressida has told the truth in her original appearance, and that her hesitations in this last appearance are equally genuine. Between those two glimpses she has shown us the inside and outside of her character once more. Her heartbroken outburst when she learns of her fate seems perfectly natural under the circumstances. When she vows to Pandarus not to leave Troy, we can assume that she expects the complicity of Troilus in keeping that vow. Her last few remarks before she is turned over to Diomedes sound like the confused queries of a child in shock.

Troilus's first intimation of concern about her constancy in Act IV Scene IV grows into a dawning awareness of reality. First she shows surprise in, "O heavens, 'be true' again?" Then "O heavens, you love me not." His admonition not to be tempted brings the direct question, "Do you think I will?" And finally, her last, sad, confused question before he turns her over to Diomedes: "My lord, will you be true?"

Two men argue about her as if she were not there, Troilus accusing the Greek of shaming him by praising her, and Diomedes replying that he'll satisfy his lust with her in his own good time. How, then, might anyone be expected to behave when subjected to such indignity? Cressida, when next we see her, has gathered her strength and retreated behind the facade that protected her prior to her affair with Troilus. She uses her skill to maintain what dignity she can, giving the Greeks back exactly what they give her. How much easier it is to put on the armor of callousness and pretend to be unmoved by the physical violation of the Greek kisses than to succumb to the role of victim and admit to the symbolic rape.

In *The Demon Lover*, her fascinating study of terrorism, Robin Morgan discusses the phenomenon of psychological bondage between captor and captive.[5] The tendency for the captive to form an affective bond with the captor, whether erotic or otherwise, is common. Stories of pioneer women who became the wives of their Native American captors abound, as do tales of similar liaisons. Surely that tendency would be all the stronger when the victim is not stolen but is turned over to her captives as part of a negotiation.

Seen in this light Cressida's behavior becomes both plausible, and psychologically probable. Her fits and starts, as she argues, pleads, and finally gives in to Diomedes's demands, give another glimpse of the girl who first confessed to her love for Troilus. To be sure, her last speech defines the Renaissance idea of woman as a creature ruled by physical passion. But Cressida, as Shakespeare's conscious creation, is merely describing herself as she appears in men's eyes. "Ah, poor our sex!" she cries, "this fault in us I find,/The error of our eye directs our mind" (V.ii, 109-10). How this differs from men, we never learn, but Cressida accepts the blame that society has taught her is hers by right. She goes on to the next man because the last one turned her over to him with the fear and expectation that she would be untrue. It was a self-fulfilling prophecy, and one that justifies Troilus's societally induced convictions of man's superiority to women.

Troilus is freed from his thralldom to love and in his last appearance seems determined to extract some sort of retribution from Diomedes, not for Cressida, but for his horse. Cressida has become old news, the prize gained, lost and easily forgotten because she never had any reality for Troilus to begin with. She was simply the object of his anima projection, and once it is no longer possible to imagine her as the embodiment of that anima, she loses all value for him. If Troilus, or any other member of this male society, were capable of integrating his anima, he would then be able to see women as human beings, as individuals with their own characteristics, not merely as projections from his own unconscious.

Cressida, in marked contrast to the male characters surrounding her, seems to live her life much more consciously. She is aware of her own foibles or to put it another way, her own shadow. While there seems to be an element of animus projection in her love for Troilus, there is no trace of self-deception when she turns from him to Diomedes. When she replies, in answer to his question about the owner of the sleeve, "'Twas one that lov'd me better than you will," love is in the past tense for her. It is with regret and sad resignation that she turns away from love to mere physical passion. She is, as is so often remarked, a frankly sensual woman, who is able to enjoy a sexual relationship with much the same sense of reality that Diomedes himself does. In that sense, perhaps Cressida has begun to integrate her own animus in order to live in a world that is not designed for the kind of woman she might be under different circumstances.

In this respect, Cressida excites so much male dismay for the same reason that we shall see Helena do in *All's Well*. She behaves like a man, and that is, after all, a cardinal sin. Although it is an accepted thing that women are inferior beings, the most serious crime they can commit, it would seem, is to behave like men instead of like themselves.

What, then, is regarded as proper male behavior in this world? Who are these Trojans who will fight to the death to keep the foreign Helen from her lawful spouse, while calmly turning Cressida, one of their own, over to the Greeks without a second thought? Who are these Greeks who devote their lives to the cause of the weak Menelaus, whose silly wife has chosen to stay with another man?

Consider first Agamemnon, the Greek general who should, in a properly ordered world, be the moving force in this action. Essentially ineffectual, he has allowed this pointless war to continue for seven long years while his troops have become restive and undisciplined. Although Ulysses praises him ostensibly, the "absence of degree" or breakdown of the hierarchy that has occasioned the Greek failure can only be attributed to Agamemnon's weak, indecisive leadership.

Priam likewise appears to be inconsequential in his effects on the Trojan efforts. He makes only the briefest of appearances, the most telling of which is to urge his son Hector to stay out of his fatal battle. Thus we see two leaders who should, in Jungian terms, represent the self but who, instead present only a vacuum in the center of each camp.

Hector and Ulysses, despite their relative competence, do not fill that vacuum because they too are corrupted by the vapidity of their causes, locked into the adolescent pattern of the hero. The traditional path of the hero, seen in Jungian terms, as a metaphor for male individuation proceeds from the successfully completed quest to a return home, where he takes the place of the father/king and rules his kingdom with the wisdom gained through his exertions. This whole society is physically and psychologically arrested in an early stage of the hero's journey and thus in its individual and collective development.

Ulysses, who later completes his journey, must be considered the most nearly central figure in terms of his symbolic value to the play. He attempts against great odds to keep the hierarchical system in working order, always sensible of the chaos that will result should he lose control of the troops. Sitansu Maitra regards Ulysses as representing one extreme of the Elizabethan English psyche, placing him at the opposite pole from Falstaff, a trickster figure who embodies the forces of individualism and works against the traditional hierarchy. He makes some fascinating points about the ways in which the great artist, attuned both to the collective unconscious and the *zeitgeist*, speaks for the temper of his times:

> The political situation in England, since Henry VIII's time, had kept all classes of people on the tenterhooks of aggressive nationalism. This imparted a sort of unity beneath which lay the forces of disintegration. Ulysses and Falstaff represent these two contradictory aspects of the English psyche of the time. Glib statements about Shakespeare's support of autocracy

> or hierarchical order (political or social) are made on the strange assumption that it is the conscious area of a great artist's psyche that conditions his creative activity. Shakespeare may have been a monarchist in his consciously held view of life, but a great artist, in so far as he represents his age, unconsciously assimilates or intuits the manifold movements and currents of social life that run contrary to his own consciously held beliefs and these energy-charged psychic contents, consciously denied an outlet or expression (by the creative artist in question), stimulate the relevant archetypes in the artist's collective unconscious and cause him to raise them to the conscious level by giving them artistic expression.[6]

Maitra goes on to describe Falstaff as the trickster who cannot stand unrelieved order but must create an outlet for man's nonconformist, unsocialized nature.

So Ulysses, as a symbol of order, stands, like Cressida, as a sort of self, but lacking greater goals, he functions more as a persona, that exterior shape of order which only covers the seething passions within the psyche. Despite his intelligence and leadership, Ulysses still lacks both judgment and positive values. His speech to Achilles in the third act clearly states the external, relative values of this universe:

> That no man is the lord of any thing,
> Though in and of him there be much consisting
> Till he communicate his parts to others;
> Nor doth he of himself know them for aught,
> Till he behold them formed in the' applause
> Where the' are extended; (III.iii, 116-20)

It is only the applause of others, no inner conviction of the self, that signifies the worth of a man for Ulysses. The hero or the princess requires applause, the reflection of others' esteem or envy in order to value themselves. This is a form of narcissism prevalent in the universe of this play. Lacking a conviction of self-worth, each person must constantly seek approval in the mirror of other eyes: again, the repeated theme of the external object in place of an internalized, integrated sense of self.

Ulysses, on the other hand, knows full well the fleeting nature of fame when he speaks of Time "like a fashionable host" who

> . . . slightly shakes his parting guest by th' hand
> And with his arms outstretch'd as he would fly
> Grasps in the comer . . . (III.iii, 165-68)

He frustrates us, this giant among midgets in whom we want to put our trust. Then, just as we begin to think that here, indeed, is a man worthy of the name, he commits some act of supreme insensitivity, like consigning Cressida to the role of prostitute and treating her accordingly.

Perhaps that is why Ulysses continues to hold the interest of succeeding generations. His ability to kindle hope and extinguish it in banality reminds us too sharply of all the buried heroes in the graveyards of our individual and collective hopes.

He and this play certainly have held the attention of our own century to a much greater extent than they did preceding ones. It has been observed by many commentators that this modern and postmodern world responds most readily to a play that satirizes the traditional glamour of love and war. These Greeks and Trojans have a lot to say to a time that grows ever more cynical about nationalistic power struggles in the name of honor and glory.

So if Ulysses, like his opposite number, Hector, functions as a "sort of self," embryonic at best but mostly as a persona, how do we categorize the other warriors in this charade? Achilles of course, is all ego, untempered by any sense of responsibility. He and his friend Patroclus have withdrawn from a society they no longer respect, but in so doing have lost their own sense of duty to any cause. Again, narcissism plays a large part in their relationship. Patroclus exists more as a mirror for Achilles than as a person in his own right. It is only when that mirror is finally broken that Achilles breaks out of his self-involvement and plunges back into battle, but he has, by then, lost any sense of integrity, even as a warrior. His cowardly murder of Hector is the most chilling and most damning act of the play, and serves as the ultimate act of corruption in a corrupt society.

As a valiant warrior gone bad, Achilles also represents the shadow side of both Ulysses and Hector. Hector is therefore quite literally killed by his own shadow when he murders a passing Greek for his armor and takes off his own armor in order to put on the spoils. He is killed by his own greed and self-involvement, or his shadow, personified by Achilles.

In this house of mirrors we see much doubling, redoubling, and shadow images that overlap each other. Ajax also enters the picture as another shadow-double of the warrior in his *Miles Gloriosus* incarnation. Muscle-bound, laughably stupid, and the butt of much humor, Ajax emerges nonetheless as a valiant fighter who gets the better of Hector, yet is chivalrous in accepting the truce that Hector proposes. This theme of appearance versus reality, of the frog-prince, of Beauty's beast, is underscored strikingly in Thersites's description of him as "a very land-fish, languageless, a monster" (III.ii, 264).

Perhaps Ajax, the undervalued monster, is the ancestor of Caliban, that painful reminder of our human tendency to punish those sports of nature in our midst.[7] And who leads the pack in such cases, but the trickster, in one of his more repulsive roles. Here we meet him as Thersites, himself one of nature's mistakes, who eases his own pain by picking the scabs of humanity. The trickster here is seen in his role as collective shadow, that primitive, undeveloped, unsocialized part of the unconscious that breaks forth in the cruelty of children when they choose a scapegoat. His language is like an eruption of the festering anger within this society, possibly of the foot soldiers themselves, who are mere pawns in this foolish game of chess. We might find his modern equivalent in the heavy metal and punk bands that have served as an outlet for the anger of some segments of the adolescent population.

Thersites is very different from the carnival figure of Falstaff, whom Maitra characterizes as the trickster embodiment of Shakespeare's society. This twisted, vicious clown wishes only to destroy any trace of happiness or satisfaction in those around him. He is, like Iago, a chaos figure, whose sole aim is destruction and misery. His appearance as a chorus, then, commenting on all the other characters, is one of the play's most disconcerting but ultimately reassuring devices. Eventually we come to accept him in his chorus role as the voice of reason after all. His vituperation is an honest commentary on this polluted society, and his remarks are undeniably funny to boot. He inserts himself between the audience and the characters like one of Brecht's *verfremdung* devices, thus alienating us, and allowing us to maintain an emotional distance from the action.

Pandarus, with his unctuous, lip-smacking advertisements for sex, is only a more refined version of the vulgar Pompey in *Measure for Measure*, appealing to man's more prurient, less mature nature. The doubling continues with him and Thersites, as each other's shadow selves. Thersites's execrations, vile though they are, are more honest than the contrived efforts of Pandarus to romanticize and sugarcoat what is ultimately only a sexual encounter. The infantile nature of Troilus's passion is most tellingly underscored in the baby talk of Pandarus on the morning after: "Would it not, a naughty man, let it sleep? A bugbear take him!" (IV.ii, 32-33).

Adelman notes in her essay[8] that Pandarus, after he has brought the two together in what seems to be mutual desire, altogether deserts his niece emotionally and aligns himself with Troilus. Cressida has become, as clearly to her uncle as to the rest of the men in the play, merely an object and now, for his present purposes, a used object that ceases to hold any interest for him.

One of the play's cruelest moments is when Pandarus is informed of Cressida's status as trade for a hostage and he gives not one second of thought to her feelings. "The young prince will go mad.," he moans, ignoring her fear and sorrow and thinking only of his own advancement gone sour.

Troilus, meanwhile, has shown himself undeserving of anyone's concern by his own self-centered reaction at the news. "How my achievements mock me," he cries, presumably in one phrase reducing Cressida, yesterday's queen of his heart, to last night's "achievement." Cressida may well say, "Ah, poor our sex," when she surrenders to Diomedes. She allowed herself to believe in love for a moment, to her own later undoing. Only stubborn realism and intelligent insight allow her to survive as a person amid this institutional reification of her as object only.

Again she emerges as a far more mature individual than the men around her. She has integrated not only both shadow and animus but she has proved herself capable, at least to some extent, of determining her own value, rather than relying solely on the "applause" Ulysses deems necessary for definition of self-worth. She values herself to the extent that she survives in whatever way she is able, which is through men, bravely and without illusion.

Who is left, then, in this tattered band, to fit into our puzzle? The ancient warrior Nestor, like Ajax, owes something to the stock tradition of the Atellan farces, precursor of the commedia dell arte, in which many archetypes found their enduring theatrical incarnations. Nestor is a typical Pantalone character, the foolish, garrulous old man who has never outgrown the mentality of his youth. Very often this character is endowed with a young wife who cuckolds him with a younger man. In this comedy of arrested development Nestor is emblematic of his society's plight. His wheezing braggadocio may be amusing, but it furnishes a grim preview of things to come for those who ignore "that old common arbitrator, Time," and attempt to remain in the hero's trap forever.

Much has been written about the Trojan bias of this play, based on the emphasis Shakespeare places on the courtly behavior of the Trojans. Aeneas, a minor character, performs the important function of symbolizing this Trojan concern for chivalric honor. Charles Boyce makes the point that "Shakespeare and his contemporaries saw Aeneas as an ancestor figure because his great-grandson Brut was thought to have settled England and founded London as New Troy."[9]

Aeneas acts as herald and emissary to the Greeks, greeting Diomedes with exquisite courtesy when the latter comes to carry Cressida off to his camp.

> . . . In humane gentleness,
> Welcome to Troy! Now, by Anchises' life,
> Welcome indeed! By Venus' hand I swear,
> No man can love in such a sort
> The thing he means to kill, more excellently,
>
> (IV.i, 21-25)

Diomedes responds in kind, and we see once more that war is a game to these boy-men. The reason for the fight is not important, but only the fight itself, which gives them all a reason for continuing the hero's game. It is not difficult to understand Troilus's self-deception and romanticizing of his feelings for Cressida when this is the kind of atmosphere in which he has learned his values.

This Trojan bias, can, of course, can be emphasized or de-emphasized in the theatrical production. A recent production at Yale Repertory Theatre was directed by Adrei Belgrader, who is best known as a director of farce. As is consistent with his style, Belgrader chose to make the whole play as broadly exaggerated as possible. The Greeks were mindless muscle men, strutting, flexing, and indulging in crude insults. The Trojans, in sharp contrast, displayed an Oriental bent for luxury and ceremony, more concerned with the seating arrangement in their counsels than with winning the war. Helen was a blonde floozy of the brainless starlet type, and Patroclus was an effeminate homosexual "wife" to Achilles. Thersites was a street ruffian who worked the audience like a carnival barker, and Pandarus was, like Patroclus, an extremely effeminate but rather sympathetic figure. Only Troilus and Cressida functioned as figures of relative humanity among the caricatures around them. The result was to make both sides ridiculous, of course, and to show the impossibility of natural love in so perverse a setting.

The production was interesting but, by choice, lacking in the subtleties and ambiguities that have made the play so intriguing to twentieth-century audiences. What it did very effectively was to focus on the principle that any virtue carried to its extreme becomes a vice. Archetypally, all the warriors on both sides merely represent various aspects of the hero. He is fierce, proud, gallant, humble, chivalric, brave, and loyal at his best. Taking those qualities to their extreme, he becomes savage, conceited, affected, foolhardy, and blind.

The last two of these characteristics become painfully evident in the third scene of Act V, when Hector defies all the voices of reason and intuition to go forth to his death. Here we see the hero, all rampant ego, ignoring his anima in Andromache, his intuition in Cassandra, and even the voice of the father, of seasoned wisdom, in Priam.

Hector is a man who at one time appeared to be farther along the path than Ulysses in his ability to assign value according to his own inner imperatives. Early in the play he cautions the young Troilus against overvaluation of the object:

> But value dwells not in particular will,
> It holds his estimate and dignity
> As well wherein 'tis precious of itself
> As in the prizer. 'Tis mad idolatry
> To make the service greater than the god,
> and the will infectiously itself affects,
> Without some image of the' affected merit.
>
> (II.ii, 53-60)

Thus Hector, who came so close to reason, growth, and sanity, to the ideal warrior-hero, is wiped out by his departure from his own ideals. Caught up in the madness of battle, he is ultimately responsible for his own death through uncharacteristically greedy and careless behavior. The wild wail of Cassandra, the exiled female will, cries for all of Greece and Troy in a last farewell to the dead hero:

> O, farewell, dear Hector.
> Look how thou diest, look how thy eye turns pale.
> Look how thy wounds do bleed at many vents,
> Hark how Troy roars, how Hecuba cries out,
> How poor Adromache shrills her dolors forth.
> Behold, distraction, frenzy, and amazement,
> Like witless antics, one another meet,
> And all cry, Hector! Hector's dead! Ho Hector!
> (V.iii, 80-87)

Hector is dead, and with him all of Troy's hope, and the rest is merely an unsavory picture of Greek triumph.

The last word, though, belongs to Pandarus, as Shakespeare takes us forcibly away from any emotional involvement with his characters. Pandarus, it seems, is also dying, from the well-earned ailments of his trade. But his chilling legacy, bequeathing us his diseases, seems to hold more horrors than a catalog of physical ills resulting from the "hold-door trade." Surely this play speaks of all the ills both flesh and spirit are heir to in a world whose physical corruption is only the outward manifestation of the soul-sickness within.

We can choose to reject that legacy by changing our focus, just slightly, to see what archetypal constellations we may have missed. Cassandra's gift of prophecy, according to myth, came from Apollo, the champion of reason and the spirit, who stands in direct opposition to the Dionysian principles of the irrational, of disorder, in short, of the trickster. This society that has descended into its animal elements has lost not only its soul, or anima component, but the corresponding masculine principle of spirit. Cassandra incorporates both those higher principles in her sibylline status, which confers a sort of androgyny upon her.

That concept of androgyny was present in the early Gnostic sects, which included in their trinity the female Sophia who, as the principle of wisdom, breathed spirit into the world, thus bringing the masculine and feminine principles into harmony. Later Christianity exiled Sophia and substituted the Holy Ghost for an all-male Trinity, supplemented by the Virgin Mary.[10]

Jung, product of the patriarchal world that he was, discusses the archetype of spirit almost solely in masculine terms,[11] despite his own interest in early Gnosticism, so this application of the archetype to Cassandra is based on a post-Jungian, less rigidly gender-based view than his world would have permitted.[12]

Ultimately the battle these warriors are waging is against themselves, and Cassandra symbolizes all that they are seeking to ignore. They have exiled both their animus and their rational, intuitive and reflective functions, leaving only men of action, toy soldiers who just keep on marching, wenching, and fighting.

And so, though Troilus says, "Hector is dead; there is no more to say," he is misguided as usual. There is much to say and much to do. The Hector within us needs to die, in order to allow us to grow and mature, to get beyond the hero's journey so that we can begin our inner journey toward the self.

Chapter IV

Bewitched, Bothered, and Bewildered: The Anima as Trickster in *All's Well*

> The web of our life is of a mingled yarn, good and ill together: our virtues would be proud, if our faults whipt them not, and our crimes would despair, if they were not cherished by our virtues. (IV.iii, 71-74)

Although *All's Well That Ends Well* shares many of the qualities that characterize the other two "bitter" comedies, it is distinguished by a singularly unsympathetic hero and, for many, an equally unappealing heroine. Angelo, despite his initial hypocrisy, is redeemed by his repentance, as is Isabella by her mercy. We can feel compassion for both Troilus and Cressida, caught in the web of a corrupt society. Bertram, on the other hand, rich, powerful, and blessed with loving guidance, seems to be an incorrigibly dishonest, spoiled brat. As for Helena, her unrelenting and, some would argue, unprincipled pursuit displays an incredible insensitivity and frighteningly single-minded urge to have her own way, despite the wishes of her husband/victim.

They young lovers are, in fact, so implausible that they furnish the material for rather broad, almost farcical comedy. There is undeniably, as has been suggested, a fairy-tale quality to the plot,[1] like its source in Boccaccio. What makes the play unusual is its parodic quality. Bertram and Helena are caricatures, like the characters in *Once Upon a Mattress*, Mary Rodgers's lighthearted musical parody of "The Princess and the Pea."[2] Helena, like Winifred, is not the gossamer-brained, swooning maiden that the hero prince/knight seeks to win. She is, rather, a dogged and, at times, apparently humorless huntress.

In typical male fashion, this preposterous woman decides that she will get her man by valiant deeds, rather than by passive vigil. That in itself is not uncommon in Shakespeare, whose boy/girl adventurers are among his most well-loved creations. But Helena is different in that she never employs the more traditional means of gaining his love by winning his admiration in another persona, like the wistful Viola/Sebastian or the saucy Rosalind. She does not seek Bertram's love in the usual female fashion because she appears to think like a man, not a woman. Her actions suggest she believes that if she wins possession of him, by whatever means, he will be hers.

Under the circumstances it is not surprising that Bertram runs as fast and as far as he can. What is surprising, even completely implausible, is that she wants him in the first place, this foolish, unkind, and misogynistic boy.

That Bertram *is* a boy, and not a man, seems to be of the utmost importance here. It must certainly have been a critical point for Shakespeare, who mentions the character's youth numerous times in his text. Charles Boyce notes and documents that fact convincingly:

> Bertram's youth, another plausible excuse for his folly, is repeatedly referred to. He is in his "minority" (4.5.69), a ward of the King, who feels he is too young to be a soldier. Lord Lafeu is asked to advise him for he is "unseason'd" (1.1.67). When he rejects Helena, the King calls him a "proud, scornful boy" (2.3.151), and when his mother learns of his flight, she calls him a "rash and unbridled boy" (3.2.27). Even Parolles describes him as "a foolish, idle boy", "a dangerous and lascivious boy", "that lascivious young boy" (4.3.207, 212, 290). In 5.3 the Countess asks the King to forgive Bertram his "natural rebellion done i' the' blade of youth" (5.3.6), and he himself confesses to having seduced Diana "i' the' wanton way of youth."[3]

Thus, in archetypal terms, we clearly have what Jung would call a *puer*, who if not rescued from his own inclinations, might easily become the *puer aeternus*. This young man has not even made it to the hero stage, which is the first station on the individuation journey. The *puer aeternus* retains the psyche of an adolescent, regardless of his chronological age. Our own era, with its fixation on youth, produces this specimen in sad abundance, along with its counterpart, the *puella aeterna.* Selfish, concerned only with pleasure, adventure, and appearance, these people pursue what Jung has called the provisional life, frequently attempting to renew their own youth by seeking ever-younger partners to maintain their self-delusion.

Of this type, Jolanda Jacobi writes:

> In spite of his age he has no ego-stability and is miles away from the realities of life. So long as these defects are not removed it is better not to take too deep a plunge into the myth haunted depths of the soul or to gallop away on a stout spiritual Pegasus - one could easily become the victim of inflation and lose the earth altogether from under one's feet.[4]

Bertram clearly needs help if he is to find his way toward manhood. How does Helena fit into the role of helper here? Unlike the Duke, she cannot be construed as the self, and she is certainly no ordinary anima figure because she is much too masculine in her behavior. Her outstanding assets appear to be arcane skills that verge on the magical and a decided flair for deception and conspiracy. These are clearly the characteristics of the trickster, in yet another of his/her many guises.

The trickster, according to Jung,[5] emerges as perhaps the most complicated of all the archetypes. In his better known roles, he can appear as innocent prankster or as a more sinister deceiver. Falstaff and Puck might be examples of the former; at his darkest he might take on the characteristics of an Iago, that chilling descendant of the medieval vice who wreaks chaos by his persuasive charm. Tom Sawyer is the best example of an American trickster, one who falls into the same category as *Til Eulenspiegel* or *Peer Gynt.* Every culture has its versions of what Jung categorizes as an archetype of the collective, rather than the personal, unconscious. The roots of this ancient figure are in the primitive, preconscious stage of human development, "an absolutely undifferentiated human consciousness, corresponding to a psyche that had hardly left the animal level."[6] The trickster at this level thus fills the role of collective shadow.

But the trickster continues to develop in various cultures, and we see his many other traits. As the shaman or medicine man or woman, he takes on the role of healer. In order to become such a person, it is necessary in many societies to be subjected to enormous physical and emotional punishment as part of the initiation into the magical, healing mysteries. Via this route the figure of the wounded healer emerges from the trickster myth and develops, by gradual permutation, into a savior figure.

Now the picture of Helena begins to take on more definition; as the mists clear away, we can see her role as trickster begin to coalesce. Jung might, indeed, have been describing Bertram's condition when he wrote the following at the end of his essay on the trickster:

> If, at the end of the trickster myth, the savior in hinted at, this comforting premonition or hope means that some calamity or other has happened and been consciously understood. Only out of disaster can the longing for the savior arise - in other words, the recognition and unavoidable integration of the shadow create such a harrowing situation that nobody but a savior can undo the tangled web of fate. In the case of the individual, the problem constellated by the shadow is answered on the plane of the anima, that is, through relatedness. In the history of the collective as in the history of the individual, everything depends on the development of consciousness. This gradually brings liberation from imprisonment in..."unconsciousness" and is therefore a bringer of light as well as of healing.[7]

Helena works undercover, like the Duke, as befits a good trickster figure, eventually bringing Bertram to the beginning of self-awareness, to confrontation with his own shadow and in proper order with his anima, also personified in herself.

Clearly enough, Bertram's personal shadow is the universally castigated Parolles, another *miles gloriosus* figure whose outrageous behavior also contains an element of the trickster. It is ultimately his sudden collapse into remorseful realism, or consciousness, that signals the beginning of Bertram's approaching change.

The other important archetypal characters in this drama include the Countess, who is arguably the most appealing mother in the canon, her friend, Lafeu, another wise old man, and the King, who emerges as usual as an icon of the self.

Diana and her mother parallel Helena and her adoptive mother, the Countess, in an appealing incarnation of the *Kore* myth, with Demeter and Persephone, a theme that is also prominent in two of the romances, *The Winter's Tale* and *Pericles*.

What then of Lavatch, the clown who would seem to fall into the already crowded trickster category in this play? As a not particularly savory legacy of the recently deceased Count, he might well symbolize the shadow side of that gentleman, his late master, and explain, in some sort, much of Bertram's character, which seems incompatible with the high principles of his mother and the reported quality of his father. Shakespeare, the master psychologist, gives us some hints about Bertram's difficulties in the play's opening speech, when the grieving Countess observes that in letting her son leave home, she buries a second husband.

Bertram's instincts are sound in this respect at least. He needs to leave the nest and escape from his mother in order to grow into manhood. It is in this move that he begins to avoid the trap of the *puer aeternus*, who often remains in a permanently dependent state out of excessive fondness for the mother.

The young count leaves moreover at the call of the King, the self who summons him forth toward the quest of the hero, the young man's first step toward maturity. But this king is an endangered self, ill and discouraged by inept physicians. Like *Everyman's* neglected *Good Deeds*, he lies, so weakened and diminished that no hope is held for his recovery.

This first scene paints a wonderfully sympathetic picture of the Countess who, in addition to her obvious warmth for the two young people, also possesses the strength to stand alone and furnish them an example. She warns Helena against excessive grief in a kindly speech that both evokes and contrasts with Gertrude's remonstrance to Hamlet. Then, like Polonius, she provides her son with advice for the conduct of life, but with greater economy and less emphasis on self-interest and material benefits.

> Be thou blest, Bertram, and succeed thy father
> In manners as in shape! Thy blood and virtue
> Contend for empire in thee, and thy goodness
> Share with thy birthright! Love all, trust a few,
> Do wrong to none. Be able for thine enemy
> Rather in power than in use, and keep thy friend
> Under thy own life's key. Be check'd for silence,
> But never tax'd for speech. What heaven more will
> That thee may furnish, and my prayers pluck down,

Fall on thy head! . . .

And then going on to her friend, Lafeu, she continues:

. . . Farewell! My lord,
'Tis an unseason'd courtier, good my lord,
Advise him. (I.i, 61-72)

These are the words of a woman who lives by the precepts of Christianity in its essence, and of a mother who grieves and fears for the welfare of her headstrong, immature son. Clearly Shakespeare intends her to reflect the values and judgments deemed most laudable by his contemporary audiences.

Having introduced the Countess, he proceeds to show us Helena in two distinctly contrary moods. Her soliloquy reveals absolute infatuation with Bertram's person, his looks, and his social position, which is lamentable only because it places him above her. She sounds like a mooning schoolgirl with an adolescent crush on a popular performer. No hint of love for Bertram's personality, character, or mind enters this speech, but only praise for his physical attributes and his glamour.

The smitten adolescent disappears entirely when she enters her verbal fencing match with the man of words, Parolles. She outwits him easily, first parrying each of his thrusts on the ills of virginity, then forcing his hasty retreat when she neatly corners him on the subjects of his questionable military valor and his dandified clothing.

Human nature, if it were consistent, would scarcely allow a young woman of such obvious intelligence to dote on a shallow boy merely for his looks and position. But here, once more, we see Shakespeare's great knowledge of our inconsistency, and we are reminded anew that these characters are human beings as well as archetypal figures. Love is no respecter of logic or indeed of any other identifiable quality. Life and literature are crammed with worthy men and women who dote on unworthy and unlikely others. When Puck anoints us with his magical herbs, all reason and judgment flee. Helena has projected her animus on Bertram, and that is that. The real Bertram might as well not exist.

Helena then vows to pursue her dream in a pathetically deluded speech which sets out to defy logic as the greatest impediment to accomplishment.

> Impossible be strange attempts to those
> That weigh their pains in sense and do suppose
> What hath been cannot be. Who ever strove
> To show her merit, that did miss her love? . . . (I.ii, 224-27)

Who indeed, but most of womanhood at one time or another? Helena's logic is male, not female. The notion that stout hearts can win fair men is not only a contra-sexual idea, but it goes directly against her own knowledge of how love operates. Her infatuation for Bertram is based on looks and position, not on merit. His unavailability lends him glamour, rather than making him less desirable. He is analogous to the beautiful princess in the tower, and she is casting herself as the intrepid knight whose impossible feats will win the prize as a matter of policy. Like all the knights and helpless suitors she seeks to emulate, she seems unaware of the possibility that the prize might not return her affection. Just as surely as the Trojans and Greeks objectified Helen and Cressida, she objectifies Bertram, in an amusing sexual reversal which serves only to emphasize the absurdity of all such assumptions.

With sure and subtle precision the trickster has us in his trap. One of his more unusual attributes is the ability to change sex at will, and here we see him playing havoc with all our received notions about gender and behavior. This is not to say that Shakespeare originates that aspect of the story, which we know comes from folk and fairy tale. He merely takes an ancient, archetypal theme and humanizes it for his own and, perhaps, for all time.

Although the trickster is felt most strongly in this play and in *Hamlet*, his influence pervades all four of the so-called problem plays. Certainly, he works in full cooperation with the self, as the Duke brings Angelo to consciousness of his own humanity. In *Troilus* the whole community seems to be under his sway, in their adolescent concepts of love as epitomized by Pandar, another trickster figure.

John Beebe suggests some guidelines for recognizing the presence of this tantalizing archetype in the first paragraph of his excellent article "The Trickster in the Arts":

> What I want to discuss here are the effects of certain works of art. Particularly, I have in mind works of art like *Hamlet* or the *Mona Lisa* which have a paradoxical, ironic or ambiguous effect. Such works affect us rather in the manner of certain

> difficult people, who "get to us" with their unexpectedly unsettling impact. These works of art perplex or madden us as we try to comprehend what is being said or shown to us, yet all the while they appear to be pleading innocent of any such confusing intention. They just go on being themselves."[8]

That is precisely what is happening here. The play, and particularly Helena, "just go on being themselves," while maddening or perplexing those who try to understand them.

Meanwhile, back at the palace, we meet the King/self, who clearly commands the hearts as well as the minds of his subjects. His glowing praise of the count, Bertram's father, confirms all the good opinion that his memory seems to possess. He was brave, gallant, wise, witty, courteous to all, from highest to lowest, apparently the model of a proper man.

Young Bertram has a very large pair of boots to fill, it would seem. Once more the psychological reality of Shakespeare's characters is apparent. Long experience shows us that being the son of a good father is often easier than being the son of a great father. Even the King unwittingly makes that point when he remarks that,

> . . . Such a man
> Might be a copy to these younger times'
> Which followed well, would demonstrate them now
> But goers backward. (I.ii, 45-48)

Poor Bertram! How can a boy fill a man's place as he is expected to do?

And yet, embedded in the King's next speech is information that might provide some clues about the failings of even such a great man as the late Count:

> . . . Let me not live, quoth he,
> After my flame lacks oil, to be the snuff
> Of younger spirits, whose apprehensive senses
> All but new things disdain; whose judgments are
> Mere fathers of their garments; whose constancies
> Expire before their fashions. . . . (I.ii, 58-63)

What seems at first glance to be a perfectly normal sentiment might also be construed somewhat differently. Was Bertram's father quite naturally wishing not to live in an infirm condition, like the king, or was he expressing an unwillingness to progress past the hero stage himself? His condemnation of the younger generation seems inconsistent with a man of such generosity and maturity as we have been led to believe him. Might this paragon have been unwilling to undertake the second part of his own journey, the part that relies not on the world's accolades but on one's own inner growth?

This passage, along with his preference for the sometimes odious Lavatch, allow for the possibility that the elder Rossillion did not possess all the perfections imputed to him by his survivors. Such conjectures do not bear directly on this thesis but merely enrich the possibilities of the text, particularly for the actor or director as part of the subtext of performance. Whether Bertram's faults are the result of a too-perfect father, a subtly flawed father, or of neither does not effect the facts of his behavior. His faults, however he came by them, are his own now, and only he can cure them, but not before he becomes conscious of their existence.

The interview between Helena and the Countess presents a particularly charming view of the two women's relationship. In marked contrast to the tradition of cruel stepmother, this is the Good Mother, representative of the Great Mother herself, who accepts all worthy children as lovingly as she does her own. Helena's only fear is that the Countess will view her as sister to Bertram and therefore not as potential wife. But the Countess, whom Shakespeare has taken pains to paint with kind strokes, is not jealous of her son's love, nor does she display an unworthy concern about rank. She wants her son to grow to proper manhood with a woman who loves him, and she cherishes Helena as if she were her own.

Therein, of course, lies part of the problem for Bertram. The woman his mother regards so highly becomes a part of the trap he is attempting to escape. The hero's path leads away from the world of the mother to a virgin who is part of the larger world. His snobbery and desire to break away from the mother bond render Helena distasteful to him. What adolescent boy, after all, does not find the strange and mysterious more appealing than the familiar and predictable? Helena lacks completely the air of sexual mystery required of an anima object by a young man of Bertram's character.

For Bertram, marrying Helena represents a sort of incestuous regression. He has not yet broken away and found the independence that can come for man only after he has escaped the world of the feminine, the mother's world, and has claimed the masculine world for his own.

Nancy Chodorow writes of the male imperative to break away from that female world of infancy and childhood, an imperative that is not present for the female who can identify with the mother, the first love object of either child. Chodorow argues that the male personality is formed by the denial of that first critical maternal connection. Male anxieties about gender identification stem from this break in identification.

> Certain activities must be defined as masculine and superior to the maternal world of childhood, and women's activities must, correspondingly, be denigrated. In this sense, it is the boy and not the girl, as in the Freudian account, who must make a difficult switch--not a switch in love object from mother to father, from homosexual to heterosexual, but a switch in major identification, from identifying with the mother to identifying with the father.[9]

All of this is another way of explaining the hero's journey that is traced in the folkloric literature of every known culture. For the girl, things are much different. She identifies with and, in some sense, becomes the mother in the eternal mystery of the Kore, or mother/maiden of the Eleusinian Mysteries. That is the mystery that lies close to the heart of this play; that and the mystery of the dead father's character. Bertram has been abandoned by his father, and his journey away from childhood is a precipitate one that is bound to be fraught with danger and difficulty.

Among the many versions of the mother/maiden myth, the most familiar to our culture is the Demeter/Persephone version, in which Hades, lord of the underworld, rapes and kidnaps the innocent Persephone, leaving her heartbroken mother to grieve. Eventually Demeter wins back her daughter for part of the year and, as a result, restores grain to the land each spring. This death and rebirth cycle, along with its fertility motif and descent into the underworld, define life's journey for women in the same way that the hero' myth defines it for man. C. Kerenyi, in his joint venture with Jung, *Essays on a Science of Mythology,* discusses the various cultural variations of the story, emphasizing that the figure of the goddess became threefold in some cultures, specifically the Eleusinian version. Here, Demeter and Persephone merge with Hecate, goddess of the moon, in a cthonic triad that expresses the several aspects of the feminine.

Both men and women identified with Demeter, according to Kerenyi, because this story finally encapsulates the entire experience of life. He writes:

> The primordial god and goddess undergo endless transformations before they come together; the maiden dies, and in her place there appears an angry goddess, a mother, who bears the primordial Maiden - *herself* - again in her daughter. The scene of the drama is the universe, divided into three, just as the goddess herself is threefold: original Kore, mother, and daughter. But the universe could only come to be the scene of such a drama because man had assimilated the whole world and lent it the animation and fluidity of his own mind, or, to put it differently, because the lively and versatile spirit of man had faced the universe and permeated it with itself. The archaic attitude combines open acceptance of reality with this kind of confrontation.
>
> The fluidity peculiar to the original mythological state presupposes a oneness with the world, a perfect acceptance of all its aspects. Basing ourselves on the arcadian mythologem we said earlier that by entering into the figure of Demeter we realize the universal principle of life, which is to be pursued, robbed, raped, to *fail to understand*, to rage and grieve, but then to get everything back and be born again.[10]

It is no stretch to see echoes of this myth within the play, beginning with Parolles's glib argument against virginity:

> . . . there was never virgin [got] till virginity was
> first lost. That you were made of is metal to make
> virgins. Virginity, by being once lost, may be ten
> times found; by being ever kept, it is ever lost . . .
>
> (I.i, 128-32)

At the play's point of attack, Helena is the maiden while the Countess is the mother, grieving here for her dead husband and absent son in woman's eternal litany of loss. Helena then becomes the paradox of wife and maiden when Bertram leaves her, while the loss of the Countess becomes more complete as she repudiates her son for his unworthy behavior. Later Helena forms a new triad with Diana and her mother in which the paradox deepens. Diana remains a virgin while Helena becomes a wife, deceiving Bertram and his companions into seeing false truth. Here Helena, in a sense, becomes the goddess by her false death and resurrection, emerging from the imaginary underworld to claim her rightful place as wife and incipient mother. Meanwhile, virginity has been restored to Diana in the eyes of the world, presenting the *Kore* figure in a perpetual cycle of renewal.

According to Jung, the *Kore* represents an anima figure for men; for women, it assumes the supra-personal aspect of the self. Thus what we see in this drama is the emergence of the female self in its various parts and the beginning of anima integration for Bertram, all brought about by the machinations of the trickster.

Lafeu, of all people, is the first to make the presence of the trickster felt, as he cautiously approaches the King about Helena's claim of ability to cure him. This dignified gentleman suddenly begins to sound like a snake-oil salesman, as he teases some interest out of his lethargic monarch:

> . . . I have seen a medicine
> That's able to breathe life into a stone,
> Quicken a rock, and make you dance canary
> With sprightly fire and motion, whose simple touch
> Is powerful to araise King Pippen, nay
> To give great Charlemain a pen in's hand
> To write her a love-line. (II.i, 72-78)

The King, finally piqued into curiosity, asks, "What her is this?" He is answered, "Why, Doctor She!" (II.i, 82-83)

The skeptical King is won over to hope when it is finally he, not Helena, who begins to speak in rhyme that moves almost hypnotically toward incantation and finally is resolved by the King's complete surrender into Helena's hands at the end of the scene.

This expedition into the world of myth and magic is brought to a forceful close by the following scene, in which the Countess and her clown exchange some nonsense prior to his departure for the court. Here also is the trickster, at work in the clown but on a very pedestrian level, fulfilling yet another purpose in diverting her from her worries. Now you see him, now you don't. Which is real, the material world or the world of imagination?

In another abrupt shift Shakespeare provides the answer to the question he has just raised, again employing the good Lafeu, who opens the third scene of the act with a resonant observation on the nature of the irrational:

> They say miracles are past, and we have our
> philosophical persons, to make modern and familiar,
> things supernatural and causeless. Hence is it that
> we make trifles of terrors, ensconcing ourselves
> into seeming knowledge, when we should submit
> ourselves to an unknown fear. (II.iii, 1-6)

The rational and the irrational exist in parallel worlds, working within each of us in ways we can only attempt to understand. This play, flawed as it is dramatically, exercises that principle, presenting both worlds simultaneously, creating the disquieting liminality that is characteristic of the trickster.

Helena's oddly ambiguous performance as she chooses her husband again signals the trickster's presence. She confuses the audience or reader as much as she does the indignant Lafeu, who imagines that the men are disdaining her. The scene can be played either way, but the most likely explanation is that she is merely pretending indecision in order to avoid the appearance of considering none but Bertram.

The King, now restored to strength, acts in the place of the self here as he attempts to speak reasonably to Bertram, praising Helena's extraordinary gifts and promising to supply any rank that the snobbish boy believes is missing. Finally Bertram bows to the demands of the self, albeit reluctantly, and accepts Helena as his wife.

Immediately after Bertram's cruel rejection and grudging acceptance of Helena, his shadow, Parolles, it should be noted, is not markedly worse in his behavior than the persona Bertram represents. That fact is consistent with Jung's observation that the brighter the persona, the darker the shadow. Parolles emerges as very little worse than Bertram himself because the persona displays such negative traits. In the case of a wholly evil persona, the shadow would be the repository of the finer feelings the persona had suppressed.

Parolles's acts thus take on a sort of comic vice aspect. His verbosity contrasts with Bertram's comparative verbal economy and his braggadocio with Bertram's valor, but his main fault is that, as an older companion, he has been a bad influence in encouraging the young man's worst tendencies. He is a sort of bargain-rate Falstaff who lacks the fat knight's charm.

When Parolles insults Lafeu because of his age, Shakespeare draws a clear parallel to Bertram's insults about Helena's low rank. Parolles, in trivial imitation of the King, puns with the word "count," making light of rank and showing rudeness to the older man by denigrating his age. Lafeu immediately takes his measure and reduces him to his proper place by noting that he, Lafeu, is a man; a title age cannot confer upon the shallow pretender.

Parolles, as a shadow, is merely emphasizing the traits that Bertram exhibits when pressed. Shakespeare implies that a true gentleman must first be a true man, capable of sound judgment and proper respect. The garish outside trappings that Parolles regards as important are analogous to the empty titles that cover unworthy people. The King makes the point that Helena is one of nature's noblewomen, and that the title can follow in justice. Bertram, a young, foolish snob, is no better than Parolles, who thinks that clothes make the man.

Each is given his proper dressing down by an older, wiser man. The King, as self, attempts to call Bertram back to his proper values, while Lafeu, as the wise old man, another father/self auxiliary, does the same for Parolles, who represents what Bertram might become, without the inner resources that eventually come to his rescue.

This familiar Renaissance theme of illusion versus reality, and the false versus the true continues to act as a leitmotif throughout the play, to a greater extent than in the other three. The difference here seems to be that the balance favors good and true values. The presence of a wise, reliable older generation deserves some scrutiny because of their numbers. The Countess, as a good mother, is flanked by Lafeu, and backed by the King, ultimate authority of the self. Even Diana's mother plays her part in guiding her daughter's actions.

Perhaps, after all, that in itself accounts for much of what is regarded as the dramatic and literary failure of this play. Shakespeare seems to be dealing here with the ideal rather than the real. Because of our archetypal longings and societal expectations, we look to the elders for our guidance and wisdom. In reality our lives, both individual and collective, seem to contain far more Gertrudes, Claudiuses, Poloniuses, Nestors, Lears, and Falstaffs than they do Prosperos and Paulinas. That tension between archetypal expectations and real people is a big part of every life. In our examination of *Hamlet* we shall see that part of universal existential anguish explored to its fullest.

But Bertram is much luckier than Hamlet. His safety net is so strong that, try as he will, he cannot fall through it. Somewhere deep down we all know that this is a fairy tale told by the trickster, teasing us with what we desire, rather than telling us what we have. In addition to which we cannot help but sympathize with Bertram when he confides in Parolles: War is no strife/To the dark house and the detested wife (II.iii, 291-92). Bertram speaks for humanity here is his loathing of a forced marriage. Still, it is amusing to note that he speaks as a man who has been placed in the female role, as choice rather than chooser. The trickster is at work in earnest here, showing us reality by inversion in every case; presenting the wise guides of our dreams in place of the fallible humans who confuse our waking hours; and submitting us to the shock of seeing sexual politics reversed.

The Countess claims her rightfully sympathetic role when she reads her son's headstrong letter and later when she learns of Helena's departure. Here, in the character of *Mater Dolorosa*, or Demeter, we feel once more the echoes of that ancient grief that stretches back as far as history: eternal woman, as vessel of creation and instrument of nurture, eternally sorrowing for the losses that dominate her life. To Helena, in angry sorrow, she says:

> . . . He was my son;
> But I do wash his name out of by blood,
> And thou art all my child. . . (III,ii, 66-68)

And then, after Helen's departure, the bitter truth comes out to her steward:

> . . . Which of them both

Is dearest to me, I have no skill in sense
To make distinction. Provide this messenger.
My heart is heavy, and mine age is weak;
Grief would have tears, and sorrow bids me speak.
(III.ii, 38-42)

It is significant that the most famous act of Solomon, whose name is a symbol for wisdom, was to rely on mother love to save the life of a child. As a woman, the Countess will continue to love her son, regardless of his behavior, but she will love the young woman who has become like a daughter to her too. As an archetype of the unconscious, the good mother cherishes her son's anima as a part of himself that must be realized.

Helena in turn demonstrates the anima side of her character, as opposed to the trickster aspect, in her sorrowful soliloquy upon learning of Bertram's defection. She, like his mother, is eternally compassionate and loving, demonstrating the most positive qualities of the anima, the qualities he, in his headlong flight from the feminine, is attempting to avoid. He expresses that determination clearly in his speech to the Duke of Florence, as he theatrically pledges his allegiance to the cause:

This very day,
Great Mars, I put myself into thy file;
Make me but like my thoughts, and I shall prove
A lover of thy drum, hater of love. (III.ii, 8-11)

He will be a hater of love, of eros, which is the feminine quality of relatedness. Bertram wants to escape his anima for the same reason that most young men do, because he needs to be sure of his manhood before he can feel safe in integrating the woman within him.

The Widow of Florence and her daughter, Diana, are immediately sympathetic to the unknown Helena's cause because Bertram has shown his true colors by attempting to seduce the virginal Diana. When the troops pass, Diana characterizes Bertram as "handsome" but "dishonest," an interesting use of the word in the sense that it is usually reserved for women. Diana further demonstrates her judgment by characterizing Parolles as a "vile rascal" who should be poisoned, a course she undoubtedly seizes on as a natural choice for a Florentine.[11]

Bertram's shadow confrontation begins in earnest when his companions persuade him to test Parolles by forcing him into action, daring him to win back the regimental drum. When he asks if they believe he could truly have been so deceived, the Second Lord answers without equivocation:

> Believe it, my lord, in mine own direct knowledge,
> without any malice, but to speak of him as my
> kinsman, he's a most notable coward, an infinite
> and endless, an hourly promise-breaker, the owner
> of no one good quality worthy your lordship's
> entertainment. (II.iv, 7-12)

The case is strengthened further by the First Lord, who reminds Bertram that such a companion is, among other things, a dangerous colleague in war.

Bertram is lucky in his companions. These comrades-in-arms might be regarded, from a post-Jungian perspective, as animus figures. Although Jung dealt only with the contra-sexual figures of animus and anima, contemporary scholarship admits to the possibility of same sex models within the unconscious. These figures, like their contra-sexual parallels, can be positive or negative, depending upon the situation or individual who awakens them and causes the contents of the unconscious to be projected upon them.

Parolles, the shadow, begins to come into the light in his soliloquies, which occur in the second scene of the fourth act. When alone, he admits to cowardice and laments the tongue that gets him into so much trouble. In this and in his succeeding scenes Parolles becomes, like Falstaff, in some respects a more sympathetic character than his persona. That fact is not inconsistent with what Jung and Shakespeare both knew about the dark side of the human soul. Through our shadow selves, the Falstaffs and Parolles within us, we are able to be fully human and to see, through our own flaws, both the divine and the profane in human nature. As the First Lord puts it, when he learns of Helena's false death:

> The web of our life is of a mingled yarn, good and
> ill together: our virtues would be proud, if our
> faults whipt them not, and our crimes would despair,

if they were not cherished by our virtues. (IV.iii, 70-74)

Bertram's anger and humiliation when he hears Parolles's real opinion of him brings him forcibly into contact with reality. The brave young commander is pronounced a foolish, ruttish, lascivious boy, a lecher who "gobbles up virginity, like a whale." We hear little from Bertram now until the last unconvincing moment.

We hear nothing form Bertram because, as usual, Parolles is still the repository of words. In his final speech of Act IV, the braggart shadow collapses and becomes honest with himself:

> Yet am I thankful. If my heart were great,
> 'Twould burst at this. Captain I'll be no more,
> But I will eat and drink, and sleep as soft
> As captain shall. Simply the thing I am
> Shall make me live. Who knows himself a braggart,
> Let him fear this; for it will come to pass
> That every braggart shall be found an ass.
> Rust sword, cool blushes, and, Parolles, live
> Safest in shame! Being fool'd, by fool'ry thrive!
> There's place and means for every man alive.
> (IV.iii, 331-39)

"The shadow knows," to quote an old saw. Sometimes it takes a while for the persona to catch up. Bertram is still struggling for the courage to admit his faults publicly. It is with conscious villainy, rather than self-deception, that he attempts to elude the consequences of his acts in the play's frustrating final scene. He has confronted the shadow and sees himself for what he is. Now all that remains is the courage to own his past mistakes and begin the journey toward integration.

In many ways this play might be viewed as a continued exploration of the issues in *Troilus and Cressida*, which was written just a year earlier. But while the issues are similar, the point of view is radically different. Perhaps Shakespeare's own anima, disturbed by her experience with Cressida, rose up and demanded equal time in this work of female rebellion. Certainly we can hear her voice clearly in Diana's bitter reflection on male deception. Unlike so many of Shakespeare's women Diana has a mother to warn her about the danger of trusting men's words:

> My mother told me just how he would woo,
> As if she sate in's heart. She says all men
> Have the like oaths. He had sworn to marry me
> When his wife's dead; therefore I'll lie with him
> When I am buried. Since Frenchmen are so braid,
> Marry that will, I live and die a maid.
> Only in this disguise I think't no sin
> To cozen him that would unjustly win. (IV.ii, 69-76)

There exists in this play and in *Measure for Measure,* which came immediately after it, a sense of sisterhood that is unusual and arguably unique in the canon. In both plays an anima figure becomes the agent of change and eventual integration. The other striking similarity is of course the rather odious bed-trick that so troubles contemporary audiences. Returning to the Demeter/Kore myth, however, the bed-trick becomes an act of ultimate subversion to a phallocentric culture that subjugates and objectifies women in an equally cynical way. In discussing their plot, Helena muses sadly to the widow, "But O, strange men!/That can such sweet use make of what they hate" (IV.iv, 21-22). Subversion has always been one of the only weapons of the underclass, and like all covert operations it degrades, in some sense, both perpetrator and target, possibly because it is the work of the trickster in his role of collective shadow, reminding us of our old, primitive roots.

That principle is illustrated still more forcibly in the person of Lavatch, the unhappy clown. Near the end of Act IV he makes his final, rather puzzling appearance in a short verbal joust with the dignified Lafeu, identifying himself as a "woodland fellow" who serves the prince of darkness. It is here that the Countess explains his continued presence in her household because he was a favorite of her husband, the late Count.

What is the trickster up to here, subverting and undermining the sense of honor and decorum in this noble house? Why did the Count want him there, if not to play out his own shadow role for him? Lafeu and the Countess admittedly like him well enough too, possibly because he discharges that duty for them as well. They can maintain their facade of propriety while laughing at the pranks of a hired fool, whose jokes, like Pagliacci's, might conceivably cover an unrecognized pain.

If, as some scholars suggest, children act out their parents unrealized desires, Bertram certainly fits that picture. His father had Lavatch, and he chooses Parolles, two decidedly unwholesome companions. Bertram's behavior can be read as compensation for his father's restraint or as repetition of his father's unpublished behavior. Either way, Parolles and Lavatch are a mixed pair of shadow/clowns for father and son.

Bertram's last stand, like Custer's, collapses not from change of heart but from sheer force of numbers. The young Count attempts to clear himself at every turn until the anima reappears in Helena, and he is beaten. His stubborn and consistently perfidious behavior up until that moment makes him a very poor hero indeed, considered realistically. Even the fairy-tale atmosphere of the last scene does not redeem him, but merely raises further questions about not-so-happy endings for the heroine.

Considered archetypally, though, the picture changes completely. Parolles, now reformed and accepted by the generous Lafeu, has stepped completely out of his shadow role. Temporarily Bertram, like Angelo after him, has become his own shadow. His sudden collapse at Helena's appearance takes on the color of a sinner finally freed from the burden of his sins by a a manifestation of divine grace.

That reading is entirely consistent with Helena's role as trickster/healer/savior. She has symbolically risen from the dead in an ancient archetypal theme of salvation and resurrection. Furthermore she rises, not like Christ or Osiris, but like Persephone, released form the dark prison of the underworld to the light, the eternal Kore, both virgin and mother contained in herself.

Having discovered the outline of this archetypal drama within a difficult dramaturgical puzzle, how might a director go about defining that outline more clearly? This play needs to be, as was suggested earlier, treated as the comedy it was intended to be. In order to forgive Bertram, the audience must see him as the confused and generally unpleasant adolescent that he is. The actor should be very young and handsome, definitely a boy, not a man, the *puer aeternus*, about to embark on the adventure of life.

Now, what is the ultimate symbol of adventure for a young Frenchman seeking fame, glory, and asylum in foreign territories but the Foreign Legion? The Cavalier model is also familiar, thanks to D'Artagnan and friends, but the Foreign Legion lends itself more readily to what can emerge as a rather affectionate satire on a young man's coming of age.

As for Helena, the intrepid traveler and huntress of the biggest game, she might in such a production be costumed in early-twentieth-century safari gear, with long skirt reaching to her stout boots, all surmounted by the traditional pith helmet. Having thus defined the two main characters as runaway boy and avenging anima, the comedy of adolescent rebellion becomes clear. Freed from the obligation to take them literally, we are able to enjoy what now emerges as a familiar rite of passage.

A whimsical director might take things one step further by allowing Helena to step back into her trickster role at play's end. She might give birth onstage, not to an infant, but to a pillow, which she hands to the astounded Bertram before running offstage toward freedom.

Some readers will find such suggestions heretical, but current production trends allow for much freedom in costume and setting. No other playwright has endured through such enormous changes in acting and production styles, only one more proof of Shakespeare's staying power. He invents himself anew for each generation, precisely because of the eternal archetypal values he represents. Those who regard themselves as traditionalists must first choose a tradition somewhere within the enormous scope that extends from street clothes and no scenery to the most elaborate historical realism to the pure fantasy of Peter Brook's ground-breaking *Midsummer Night's Dream*.

Bertram is the step between Troilus and Angelo. This is not an individuation drama; it is an amusing fairy tale about a boy's entry into manhood. Thanks to the benign influences around and within him, Bertram is going to grow into his title. In direct opposition to *Troilus and Cressida, All's Well* offers a model, for the integration of the feminine, and for female individuation as well. Helena represents the woman's journey into the underworld of birth and rebirth, to return triumphant as maiden/mother/Kore in the eternal cycle of life.

Chapter V

Oh Dad, Poor Dad: The Universal Disappointment of Imperfect Parents in *Hamlet*

For who, that's but a queen, fair sober, wise,
(III.iv, 189)

Where every god did seem to set his seal
To give the world assurance of a man.
This was your husband. . .(III.iv, 61-63)

Oscar Wilde suggested that perhaps the greatest question raised by *Hamlet* was, "Are the critics mad or only pretending to be so?"[1] Still, like the blind men and the elephant, we can each make some small contribution to our collective understanding, knowing that no one view can begin to encompass the play's richness. So, in the manner of pilgrims to a shrine, we set off, ragged, and unworthy, but determined to spend some time in the presence of the transcendent.

It should surprise no one that, on an archetypal level, the trickster plays the main role in this drama since, as Wilde so piquantly reminds us, it is typical trickster behavior that so confuses us about Hamlet himself. Since Freud-Jones[2] paper and the Olivier film, however, Oedipus and Hamlet have become almost inextricably entwined in the public mind, thereby overshadowing some of the play's more subtle aspects and oversimplifying its richness and depth.

The latter point provides an unusual opportunity for demonstrating the differences between Jung's and Freud's thinking, while furnishing a perfect springboard for the leap into a Jungian reading of the play.

We know that, for Freud, all psychological impulses sprang from the body, from infantile experiences of pleasure and pain that later translated themselves into more complex adult emotions. For him and his disciples Hamlet's dilemma can be reduced to mere sexual guilt and jealousy over the mother who was possessed first by his father and then by his uncle. He cannot kill Claudius because he sees himself in Claudius.

For Jung, whose break with Freud was precisely because of such reductive beliefs, Hamlet would never have been forced into so narrow and ill-fitting a mold. Man, to Jung as to Shakespeare, was not peasant slave to his bodily sensations but a piece of work noble in reason and infinite in his faculties, capable of angelic action and godlike apprehension. In short, Jung believed that man possessed a soul as well as a body, and it is Hamlet's soul with which this play has to deal.

From a Jungian standpoint the death of Hamlet's father and his mother's remarriage to his uncle represent the universal experience of parental discovery. For most people the dawning realization that parents are imperfect and sexual creatures as well, takes place during childhood and adolescence. At some point anger and disillusion result in rebellion of one kind or another, as the child makes the necessary break from parental dependency. For boys the break can be even more traumatic than for girls, because it represents the journey away from the world of the mother into the man's world, a drama that is enacted in the universal story of the hero.

For Hamlet this realization and rebellion come later than usual. He has idealized his parents who as king and queen, represent the ideal archetypal parents who are all-good and all-powerful. His father's death is both an actual and psychological event in that it represents the death of the good father of our archetypal expectations. For most of humanity this paragon is replaced by a human father at some point. In Jung's terminology we withdraw our archetypal projections and accept the reality of what turns out to be, in most cases, a good-enough father.[3]

The same process occurs with the mother of course, and although the child within us occasionally yearns for the infallible parents of early childhood, most of us come to terms with the flesh-and-blood parents of reality.

Hamlet's idealism and his privileged position have preserved his illusions overlong. He may be as old as thirty, if we are to take the grave digger literally, but in any case he is clearly past adolescence: a university student and a young man who has seen something of the world at the play's point of attack.

Claudius becomes a shadow figure for the good father who is dead. His hasty marriage to Gertrude forces Hamlet to see his mother as a sexual being for the first time. Claudius personifies all the seamy, physical reality that Hamlet had refused to see in his idealized father. He and Gertrude become the sensual parents of reality, forcing the ideal, archetypal parents of imagination to die a violent death. With Claudius dead Gertrude can return to her former imaginative status, preserved like her first husband in the museum of selective memory; father and mother, king and queen, sacred, untouchable, eternal.

This, then, is where the trickster steps once more into the breach and saves the endangered ego. Hamlet, brought suddenly and belatedly to the realization of his parents' fallible humanity, regresses to an earlier stage of his development in order to integrate the pieces that have been left behind by the courtier-scholar with his head in the clouds. The trickster makes his appearance here as the adolescent prankster, who in his dizzying swoops between childhood and manhood maintains some sense of equilibrium by manic and frequently outrageous adolescent humor.

We see the trickster in this guise on any high school or college campus. We see him in publications like *Mad* magazine, on TV programs like *Saturday Night Live*, and in films like the young Woody Allen made. He howls through dormitory halls during exam time, sometimes drinks too much, is often too loud or too vulgar, and frequently is wickedly, unspeakably funny. His irreverence saves him from feeling too much until his hormones have stabilized and he can rejoin the human race, maintaining enough of the trickster's humor to allow him to laugh more frequently than to cry. If all goes well, that happens in good time. If not, he remains in his own never-never land as *puer* or *puella aeternus*, eventually transmogrifying into an aging, desperate child for whom time has become perpetually out of joint because he has never learned to reconcile archetypal expectations with reality.

So, belatedly, the sensitive, intellectual young prince enters his trickster adolescence, armed with learning, experience, and brilliant intellectual gifts. Hamlet is not feigning madness. Rather, he is escaping madness in a fairly standard way, through the good offices of the trickster.

Where, then, do the other characters find their place on this inner stage? Ophelia, clearly enough, becomes the rejected anima who had been integrated very early in Hamlet's life as evidenced by his tenderness, compassion, and other good anima qualities. He rejects her, his soul, temporarily, when the shock occurs, denying his finer qualities because of the ghost's orders and disgust over his mother's sexuality.

Ordinarily, according to Jung, the shadow must first be integrated before we can truly integrate our contra-sexual archetype. Hamlet's shadow is Laertes, the misguided son of a foolish father, who is always capable of instant action because he is unfettered by the chains of reflection. While Hamlet is clearly an introverted, intuitive-thinking type, Laertes is an extraverted, sensory-feeling type. Laertes's character in many ways, resembles that of his father, Polonius. They are both shallow, suspicious opportunists who lack the intellectual and spiritual capacity to understand Hamlet.

This is demonstrated most convincingly in their advice to Ophelia. Neither brother nor father realizes that Hamlet's attentions stem from feelings of genuine love because they understand only what they themselves have experienced. Each projects his own qualities onto Hamlet, assuming that seduction is his goal, never understanding the purity of a relationship that is beyond their experience or capacity. It is only when Ophelia follows the false advice of these false counselors that Hamlet senses a lack of integrity in her actions and thus rejects her for the faults of others, and none of her own.

Polonius also serves as another shadow father figure for Hamlet. In this false father the prince sees all the qualities he most despises and has refused to recognize in his own parents. Polonius, usually portrayed as a comical pantalone type, is in truth a far more sinister figure. When Hamlet kills him, he succeeds in killing much of what he hates in his own father and in Claudius. It is no coincidence that he thinks he is murdering Claudius with that impetuous thrust. He is, indeed, on a psychological level murdering some aspects of the bad father he is seeking to destroy.

What about Rosencrantz and Guildenstern, that mysteriously tantalizing mixed pair that Harold Goddard refers to as "Tweedledee and Tweedledee?"[4] They emerge as another manifestation of the trickster, most appropriately as school friends of Hamlet's. One of the trickster's dazzling array of inventions is displayed most clearly in his *commedia dell 'arte* personification of Harlequin, a double-personality who is split right down the middle, each side with a different color and pattern. One of this traditional *lazzi*, or bits, is to employ this split onstage, having the two sides argue with each other, sometimes even resorting to physical combat. This of course comes from the ancient trickster legends in which the figure was able to change form and even to remove various body parts at will.[5]

The death of Rosencrantz and Guildenstern, at Hamlet's instigation, clearly represents his integration of the trickster figure. They along with Hamlet's own trickster behavior are gone when he returns to Denmark from his eventful sea voyage into the unconscious. Horatio's sweet prince is back, ready to complete the final leg of his journey toward individuation.

And what about Horatio, the last important character we must put in place before the inner drama takes form? Horatio certainly seems to be an agent of the self because of his honesty and steadfastness throughout. But perhaps what draws us to Hamlet more than anything else is that he is his own self. In him we see our own finer qualities subjected to the brutality of life. The father/king who should fill the role of self completely fails to do so in this case. Hamlet, like Ophelia, seems to be a spiritual, psychological changeling, far finer than the families into which they were born.

The self is so strong in Hamlet, as it must have been in his creator, that he searches in vain to find that inner greatness mirrored in someone or something around him. All, being human, fail to fulfill that need. He holds the mirror up to nature and is disappointed by her flaws. Only when he learns to look within, to see with the eyes of the soul, can he discern the spark of divinity that allows him to find peace.

Hamlet's first appearance, in the court, reveals him to be honest and vulnerable, without the protection of the trickster. Although his famous first line, "A little more than kin, and less than kind," shows both his eloquence and his unhappiness at the marriage, it is an aside. His remarks to both Claudius and Gertrude are beyond reproach in their tone and content. He is clearly a man in the grip of deep depression, a fact that becomes increasingly clear in his first soliloquy.

We understand now that most clinical depression is caused by loss, frequently a loss of which we are not consciously aware. The weary, flat, stale, and unprofitable world that Hamlet inhabits is not created by the natural loss of a parent, as Gertrude and Claudius suggest, but by the belated loss of innocence. If our parents are sinful, then no good can exist in the world. They have been expelled from the garden, and Hamlet along with them, his source of faith and wholeness destroyed by two deaths, those of both his good father and good mother, and with them, the possibility of all good has fled.

Therapists often become exhausted in the presence of depressive patients, who are like vacuums that suck up all the energy in their vicinity, so deep and painful is their own exhaustion and despair. This quality is apparent in Hamlet as he pulls himself with difficulty out of great pain to assert his natural courtesy toward Horatio and the two guards.

The shock of Horatio's news brings him, quite naturally, somewhat out of his despondency. Hope begins to rise once more that perhaps the good father is not completely lost to him. But this is hope tempered by fear and confusion from the beginning. Ghosts, for the Elizabethans, fell into two distinct categories for Catholics and Protestants, according to Dover Wilson.[6] For Catholics, they were actually the souls of the departed, on leave from purgatory. Protestants, on the other hand, held more complex beliefs, thinking them spirits, usually from hell but occasionally from heaven. They were thus either devils or angels who had assumed the shape of the dead.

Hamlet, then, seems to waver between the two views throughout the course of the play, but his first reaction definitely favors the Protestant view, when he vows, "If it assume my noble father's person,/I'll speak to it, though hell itself should gape" (I.ii, 243-44).

The promise of some kind of action is the catalyst needed to break, at least temporarily, the stasis that has gripped him, and he looks forward eagerly to the night, when some news may enable him to believe that the evil surrounding him may not be pervasive.

The following scene introduces, for the first time, the Polonius family together, although we have met father and son briefly in the court scene. The Hamlet that Laertes describes seems to bear no resemblance to the Hamlet we have so far seen. Still, his warning to Ophelia seems reasonable enough, given the circumstances of each. This might be merely the advice of a brother to his young and innocent sister against the danger of any young man's premature ardor. His position as Hamlet's shadow does not really come into focus here; it takes time to develop.

Then comes Polonius, whose advice appears to be sage, if a trifle stingy and overly cautious. It is not until we see the character of the old man unfold that it becomes clear how little his advice accords with his own actions. The irony of his closing remark resonates throughout the play, as we see that truth to oneself is a rare quality indeed in this place. Polonius is, as usual, mouthing platitudes that have no real significance for him. Truth to oneself translates into the basest self-interest for him, who is so far from ever knowing the self in its Jungian sense.

A picture of Polonius comes to mind, far indeed from the laughable clown of most productions and far more dangerous. We see his clones on television on any newsworthy day: perfectly tailored, handsome, white-haired, and dignified, giving their august opinions to reporters or interviewers, taking their seats in senate chambers or aboard government jets bound for the current world crisis scene. They say all the right words, and frequently, like Polonius, far too many of them, looking straight into the camera so that we can see the glint of righteous anger or the gleam of a furtive tear in their eyes. They have much to do with running the world, and they are not laughable because they are shrewd and cynical and dangerous.

How else would Ophelia and Laertes be so deceived in the quality of their father? He, like the kings he serves, wears the trappings and the suits of respectability, of the good father incarnate. But like them, he sends his children to their doom by his own foolish example. The sins of the fathers loom large in this play, and Polonius too often escapes the scrutiny he deserves as richly as do the ghost and Claudius.

The tone of his remarks to Ophelia betrays him immediately. He shows no sensitivity to her feelings, but rather berates her cruelly, calling her a green girl and a child, like Laertes judging Hamlet by his own standards of behavior. This is a typical case of shadow projection, in which we attribute to others all those qualities which we cannot or will not admit in ourselves. We can see it all around us in everyday dealings. Those who routinely suspect others of dishonesty or opportunism are those to whom it is best to give wide berth because their suspicion betrays their own inclinations.

There is a great gulf between normal caution and rampant suspicion. Both Laertes and Polonius speak as if there were no probability of true affection in Hamlet's attentions to Ophelia. One can easily conjecture about the hearts that produce that kind of suspicion. Polonius in particular does not offer prudent and compassionate warning but jumps to the wrong conclusion immediately, ordering Ophelia to cut off all contact with Hamlet. We see later that it is only when she obeys her father, rather than her own honest inclinations, that Hamlet first begins to suspect her integrity. She has never before played the games of the coquette because she is honest. As soon as she follows the advice of contrivance, she destroys the trust that has built up between them.

Shakespeare's dramaturgical mastery sandwiches the Polonius family scene between two of Hamlet's own scenes, making the contrast between their opinion and the reality all the more striking. We leave Hamlet, brooding about the possibility of hidden foulness in Scene Two, to join the spurious gaiety of a family leave-taking in Scene Three, a subtle illustration of the corruption that underlies all that occurs in the universe of this play. We rejoin Hamlet as he waits for the ghost with Horatio, commenting on the sad habit of drunkenness that pervades the court. This is surely a sober philosopher/prince, not the wanton youth of Polonius and Laertes's imagination, who reflects on the ways in which a country, like an individual, can be ruined by one fault.

Horatio first shows himself as an agent of the self when he argues strongly against Hamlet's following the ghost:

> What if it tempt you toward the flood, my lord,
> Or to the dreadful summit of the cliff
> That beetles o'er his base into the sea,
> And there assume some other horrible form
> Which might deprive your sovereignty of reason,
> And draw you into madness? . . .(I.iv, 69-74)

Hamlet's true self knows the danger is to his mind, not his body, but his ego/persona is in charge now, leading him toward the inevitable danger. Certain temptations are irresistible. We must eat the apple even if it kills us, because at that moment death appears, in Hamlet's own words "a pin's fee" compared to the torment of perpetual ignorance. Hamlet's stay in the garden has been overlong as it is.

Despite Hamlet's ecumenical confusion, the ghost seems to confirm the Catholic view of his origins when he explains that time is short, since he must spend his days in purgatory until the "foul crimes" done during his life are expiated. Clearly, this was not quite the paragon Hamlet later describes to Gertrude but a man who was cut off, by his own admission, in the "blossoms" of his sins. Poor Hamlet. The good father of his imagination is finally deader than dead. He never existed in the first place.

The ghost as spirit falls neatly into Jung's category discussion of that archetype. The spirit, which is often associated with the father, can exert both good and evil influences, as can indeed any archetype, depending upon its situation. Jung speaks of the spirit as being associated with a certain type of father complex and also as making an appearance "in a situation where insight, understanding, good advice, determination, planning, etc., are needed but cannot be mustered on one's own resources. The archetype compensates this state of spiritual deficiency by contents designed to fill the gap."[7]

In its darker and more negative manifestations, of course, the spirit can manifest itself as a ghost or as some sort of guide whose advice is ambiguous and often dangerous to the receiver. Fairy tales abound with the gnome or little old man who gives disastrous advice to the hero, only to have him either ignore it or learn some higher lesson through following the advice. Thus in the ghost, as in so many of Shakespeare's characters, the confusion of good and evil reflects and parallels life experience.

It is at this point of tension between the worlds of good and evil, childhood and manhood, reality and imagination, that the famous split occurs, when the prince's depression gives way to the mania that has inspired so much debate. He is clearly in shock when he returns to his companions, but what exactly is the cause of that shock? The fact of the murder only confirms his own intuition. The real clue as to the cause of his misery comes in his asides to and about the ghost in the remainder of the scene. While he maintains his unfailing courtesy toward Horatio and the guards, his attitude toward the ghost belies what he reports to the others about him, assuring them only that he is an honest ghost.

But "boy," "old mole," "this fellow in the cellarage," are these the expected terms for a beloved parent, a king, even an honest ghost? The trickster has come to Hamlet's rescue and removed him from an unbearable situation. Not only has the prince seen the reality of his father for the first time, but he has become aware of the grisly legacy that is his own. This warrior king, this perpetrator of foul crimes is not content with blackening his own soul. He wishes to force his son into the same trap.

Old men send young men out to fight their battles for them and to die for their quarrels. That is the story of most wars. Here we have the archetype of the father at its most pernicious, most destructive, demanding homage and patriotism, demanding the very lives of his sons in callous disregard of everything but his own selfish wishes. In *Troilus*, we see the hero as ruling archetype of a society mired in war, with old men dying for the cause of the young. Here the reverse occurs. Anthony Stevens discusses the phenomenon in detail, as it occurs in society.[8] A patriarchal society carried to its extreme becomes authoritarian and militaristic, concerned only with the perpetuation of its own power, using its citizens, rather than working for their individual and collective good.

On the other hand, a matriarchal society carried to its own extreme becomes soft, egalitarian, sensuous, and completely ungoverned. Stevens cites the counterculture of the sixties and seventies as examples of the matriarchal extreme in the United States. The eighties and nineties appear to be taking us ever farther in the other direction.

Hamlet's Denmark appears to be experiencing some similar swings of the pendulum. The warrior King Hamlet made short work of the softer Norwegian Fortinbras. The license and lechery of Claudius's court make it possible for the warlike young Fortinbras to reciprocate. Hamlet, the man of moderation; student, poet, humanist, and philosopher, finds himself trapped between a rock and a soft place. Something has been rotten in Denmark for far longer than he knew because his father was as evil as Claudius himself, in that he asks his own son to become a killer.

Harold Goddard constructs an elegant argument based on the point that Hamlet hesitates because he does not want to degrade himself to his uncle's level by becoming a murderer. Goddard refutes the notion that Hamlet's hesitation could have been based solely on a distaste for the act of killing, cautioning his reader that:

> this is to forget the atmospheric pressure to which his mind was subjected. New moralities do not spring into existence in the face of entrenched custom in full-fledged conscious and conceptual form. They begin in dumb feelings around the heart ("thou wouldst not think how ill all's here about my heart") and in momentary gleams of the imagination.[9]

What Goddard does not answer satisfactorily is why Hamlet, if moral grounds really explain his hesitation, is able to kill Polonius and speak calmly about lugging the guts into another room. Many otherwise civilized men or women might be capable of that impulsive thrust into an unseen target while under the influence of the trickster. We must not underestimate his capacity for mischief, even for evil, under certain circumstances. He is after all, according to Jung, a collective shadow, a repository of all our most ancient, primitive, amoral urges. Hamlet is, at that time, firmly in the grip of his trickster mania, bedeviled by the ghost and determined to force his mother back into the mold he has cherished, the good mother, the good, "fair, sober, wise queen" of his imagination.

As for Hamlet's subsequent lack of remorse, we can chalk that up to the trickster's score as well, but some other possibilities suggest themselves. We might argue that Polonius acts as a substitute for Claudius by dying in his place and by living as the bad father incarnate. Again, the prevalent picture of Polonius as a harmless old windbag interferes with other views of his character. He is a living monument to personal expedience, sycophancy, and disingenuousness, all qualities that Hamlet must, by his nature, abhor. He is, in short, a complete fraud but a hypocritical one, who lacks the courage of a Claudius but, as Goddard points out,[10] pours poison just as deadly into far more ears, especially those of his children.

The opening of Act II shows Polonius once more at his seamiest, as he instructs Reynaldo to spy on Laertes. This good father not only distrusts his son but does not forbear to spread a bit of scandal about him in order to learn about his activities. This is shadow projection again in a particularly loathsome guise. We need no historian to tell us about Polonius's youth. He tells us himself by his suspicions about his son. We can only pity the wife that such a man might have had, and see something of her and her life in her poor, doomed daughter.

Still Polonius like most of humanity is not evil, merely insensitive and base. He is capable at least of owning his mistakes, in the unlikely event that he perceives them. Unfortunately his limited intelligence allows him to operate only on the basis of received opinion and traditional wisdom. Upon hearing Ophelia's account of Hamlet's wild behavior, he believes it is her coldness that has made him mad. It is beyond the scope of a Polonius to understand Hamlet's pain on seeing the straightforward girl he has learned to love resort to the usual cheap sexual games of hide-and-seek. Foolish Polonius comes as close to honest humanity as he ever will when he says sincerely:

That hath made him mad.
I am sorry that with better heed and judgment
I had not coted him. I fear'd he did but trifle
And meant to wrack thee, but beshrow my jealousy!
By heaven, it is as proper to our age
To cast beyond ourselves in our opinions,
As it is common for the younger sort
To lack discretion. . . . (II.i, 107-14)

From a Jungian standpoint, this scene represents the first stage of Hamlet's rejection of his anima, the feminine side he had so easily incorporated into his psyche and that accounts for so much of what is fine in him. Goddard remarks:

> Goethe, I would say, is far closer to the mark . . .in attributing Hamlet's hesitation to a feminine element in the man. But then he proceeds to spoil it all by implying that Hamlet is weak and effeminate: "a lovely, pure and most moral nature, without the strength of a nerve that makes a hero, sinks beneath a burden which it cannot bear and must not cast away." The implication is that Hamlet ought to have killed the king at once; also that loveliness, purity, and moral insight are not sources of strength and heroism.[11]

Hamlet cannot accept faults in others because he has not yet faced the darkness within himself. He must integrate his own shadow before he can allow the anima a permanent place in his psyche, because she, being an autonomous complex like all archetypes, also has her faults. Perhaps Hamlet's hold over us stems more than anything else from his struggle to reconcile himself to a fatally flawed world, the most difficult task that any sensitive soul must attempt. Emily Dickinson, preternaturally succinct as always, summed it up in her cryptic remark, "Hamlet wavered for all of us."[12] Indeed, he wavers between heaven and hell and shows us finally that the answer is that there is no answer; only the ability to keep asking questions and to live as best we can with our choices. The rest is silence.

The appearance of Rosencrantz and Guildenstern calls forth Hamlet's trickster in ways we have not seen previously. The lighthearted student banter they evoke contrasts vividly with the seriousness of Hamlet's discourse with Horatio. Only in his soliloquies and in his conversation with Horatio, as agent of the self, do we hear Hamlet's unedited thoughts. Perhaps the most striking instance of this occurs immediately after Hamlet's encounter with the ghost, in the familiar lines

> ...There are more things in heaven and earth, Horatio,
> Than are dreamt of in your philosophy.
> But come;
> Here, as before, never, so help you mercy,
> How strange or odd some'er I bear myself--
> As I perchance hereafter shall think meet
> To put an antic disposition on-- (I.v, 166-72)

He then proceeds to implore Horatio not to reveal this ruse to anyone else. Here is the persona in communication with the self about the trickster possession that is taking place in order to save the psyche from real madness.

It is not Horatio's Hamlet, who greets his friends with crude, sexual, schoolboy humor. But these more or less well-meaning trickster figures are not prepared for the real Hamlet, who suddenly drops all pretense and pours out his heart without censor in the most moving of all his descriptions of depression:

> I have of late lost all my mirth, forgone all
> custom of exercises; and indeed it goes so heavily
> with my disposition, that this goodly frame, the
> earth, seems to me a sterile promontory; this most
> excellent canopy, the air, look you, this brave
> o'erhanging firmament, this majestical roof fretted
> with golden fire, why, it appeareth nothing to me
> but a foul and pestilent congregation of vapors.
> What a piece of work is man, how noble in reason,
> how infinite in faculties, in form and moving, how
> express and admirable in action, how like an angel
> in apprehension, how like a god! The beauty of the
> world; the paragon of animals; and yet to me what
> is this quintessence of dust? (II.ii, 295-308)

And then, the heartbreaking end: "Man delights not me--nor women neither, though by your smiling you seem to say so."

He has cast his pearls before swine in trying once more to find deeper understanding amid the shallows of his surroundings. These good fellows demonstrate the common reaction to such heartfelt confessions. They, like so much of humanity, are embarrassed by such revelations and avoid the necessity to handle such delicate material by first making light of it and then changing the subject.

Fortunately for Hamlet, the blow of disappointment is softened by pleasure at the prospect of seeing the actors once more. For the first time we see him taken out of himself by interest in the world around him. For Hamlet perhaps, as for his creator, only art has the power to transcend life's pain by shaping reality into some semblance of ordered meaning.

Even his remarks to Polonius take on a lighter, more tolerant tone, as the excitement of anticipation grips him. He is able to forgive the garrulous old man's rude and ironic interruption of the actor, whose speech he deems too long. Moreover when Polonius, with his usual officiousness, promises to use the actors "according to their desert," Hamlet demonstrates a princely charity and wisdom as he answers:

> God's bodkin, man, much better: use every man after
> his desert, and who shall scape whipping? Use them
> after your own honor and dignity--the less they
> deserve, the more merit is in your bounty. (II.ii, 529-32)

To accord even Polonius his own honor and dignity is an act that can only be performed by the true Hamlet, that self we recognize and love in him, even as it enables him to love those fallible beings who surround him.

Once the transcendent power of art, personified by the players, has left, Hamlet sinks back into the dungheap from which he has been viewing the stars. Castigating himself as a rogue and peasant slave for forgetting his cause, his language becomes baser and uglier until he seizes upon the idea of using art, rather than violence, to solve the dilemma, by forcing the king's conscience to do its work.

Here we see Hamlet's dependence upon art as salvation and furthermore some glimpse of his feelings for Claudius that belies the venom of all his former remarks. Perhaps the ghost is a devil, not his father. Perhaps Claudius, his uncle/father, is not beyond redemption. Clearly Hamlet's choice is not simply to kill but to redeem, perhaps to rediscover the goodness he seeks so desperately in those around him. Freud's Hamlet cannot kill Claudius because he sees himself in him. Perhaps Jung's Hamlet, kindlier and more complex, cannot kill Claudius because he sees the shadow of his father there, or more simply, another human being whom he cannot destroy with impunity.

When next we meet Hamlet, after the brief scene in which Polonius plans to bait his trap with Ophelia while he and Claudius observe, he has sunk, once more, into the depths. What more can be said about the "To be or not to be" soliloquy? In the BBC videotape Derek Jacobi, surely one of the twentieth century's finest Hamlets, brings each word to life, allowing us to ponder with him the universal question of choice between life and death. Which Hamlet is this? Not the trickster certainly, not the self, but the persona, beginning to understand the presence of the shadow in all its complexity. Hamlet's former bursts of self-criticism, particularly in the peasant slave speech immediately preceding this one, are directed at his inability or refusal to obey the demands of the ghost. Here we see a dawning acceptance of the traits he has formerly rejected. They are part of him, and good or bad, they remain part of him as long as he chooses to live. Hamlet has finally begun the painful process of shadow integration by owning, rather than rejecting, the parts of his personality that are not convenient.

What he does not realize at this point is that he is confusing wheat with chaff. In the very next scene comes his eloquent profession of the qualities he truly values, when he praises Horatio's temperance and lack of passionate impulse.

> . . . Give me that man
> who is not passions's slave, and I will wear him
> In my heart's core, aye, in my heart of heart
> As I do thee . . . (III.ii, 71-75)

Hamlet proves over and over that the qualities he sees in Horatio, reflection, philosophical distance, steadfastness, loyalty, and patience, are the traits that are best in himself as well. These, of course, are the very qualities for which he castigates himself. This man of thoughtful moderation, brilliant, aesthetic, studious, artistic, and compassionate, reviles himself because he is unable to be what the ghost requires, an impulsive, bloodthirsty savage.

Horatio represents the self for Hamlet, the ideal man he would become. Among all the characters in the world of this play, Horatio alone retains the prince's confidence and good opinion throughout. Only with him is Hamlet always able to reveal his innermost feelings. But consider for a moment another kind of confidant for Hamlet. Attempt to imagine his similar praise of a Laertes, a Rosencrantz, or a Guildenstern. No, Horatio is vital to Hamlet precisely because Hamlet's unerring instinct leads him to find a true mirror among the cracked and discolored glasses around him. He, unlike the fortunate Bertram, is surrounded by elders who provide no measure for his quality. He must, in order finally to find the path of individuation, both invent and pass judgment on himself. It is this lonely experience, common to so much of humanity, that we share with Hamlet, the search for authenticity amid the parody of life.

Poor Ophelia, the rejected anima, describes the prince most eloquently after the painful scene in which he takes his leave of her.

> Oh, what a noble mind is here o'erthrown!
> The courtier's, soldier's, scholar's eye, tongue, sword,
> Th' expectation and rose of the fair state,
> The glass of fashion and the mould of form,
> Th' observed of all observers, quite, quite down!
> (III.ii, 150-54)

Were he able to recognize it, the anima provides a reliable mirror, but his disgust of Gertrude, coupled with Ophelia's newly coquettish behavior, renders him unable to trust where he should.

Contrast Ophelia's description with his own painful cry, as he recounts the sins he sees in himself in the nunnery speech.

> I am myself indifferent honest, but yet I could
> accuse me of such things that it were better my
> mother had not borne me: I am very proud,
> revengeful, ambitious, with more offenses at my
> beck than I have thoughts to put them in,
> imagination to give them shape, or time to act
> them in. What should such fellows as I do,
> crawling between earth and heaven? We are

> arrant knaves, believe none of us. Go thy
> ways to a nunn'ry. (III.i, 121-28)

That posture, crawling between earth and heaven is the curse of the honest man. Because he is unable to live up to the wrong expectations, Hamlet castigates himself unjustly. Ophelia, the anima, has a far more realistic view of him than he himself does, because his view is shaped not by inner knowledge but by the false witness of the world, in particular of the father/ghost.

Hamlet's speech to the players occurs immediately before the paean to Horatio's virtues. Here we see the self firmly in control, in language and in judgment. Art speaks directly to Hamlet's self, bringing out his true qualities in a way that nothing else can. When he speaks to the players, as a good director, he is attempting to create order out of his own life's chaos.

In Lily Tomlin's brilliant one-woman show *The Search for Intelligent Life in the Universe*,[13] her main character, a bag lady, acts as tour guide to some extraterrestrials who are attempting to understand human behavior. At one point, the bag lady holds a can of Campbell's tomato soup in each hand and explains that this one is art and this is soup, or is it the other way round? She then extends the metaphor gradually to life and art as the aliens, untutored in the ways of this world, applaud the audience, rather than the players.

Hamlet's discourse on life and art contains the same observations. When he talks of actors who have "so strutted and bellow'd that I have thought some of Nature's journeymen had made men, and not made them well, they imitated humanity so abominably," is he speaking of life, of art, or of the impossibility of ever achieving the kind of merger that might satisfy the soul of the artist? Those who regard this speech as merely a way for Shakespeare to insert some of his own ideas about theatre, fail completely to understand that for Hamlet, as for Shakespeare, theatre *was* life, marred only by those too stupid or too base to play their parts with integrity.

But the true Hamlet, whom we see with the players and Horatio, disappears when the court arrives for the play. Again the trickster takes over from the self as a protective device when the pressure becomes unbearable. We see this close collaboration between trickster and self as a prominent factor in two of the other plays, *Measure for Measure* and *All's Well*, in the figure of the Duke and in the collaboration between Helena and the King. Here, however, the delicate balance is upset, and the trickster runs out of control. Goddard describes it thusly:

> Hamlet himself has o'erstepped the modesty of nature and betrayed the right of dramatic art to speak obliquely. He has produced an abortion. Forgetting that "the play's the thing," he has ruined his imaginative experiment by "telling all,"--just what he damned the players for doing, far less blatantly and offensively, in their dumb-show. He is hoist with his own petar. He has sprung the mousetrap instead of letting it spring itself, and has caught two royal mice, himself as well as the King.[14]

The trickster has tricked himself, and all Hamlet's well-laid plans are blasted not by hesitation but by the impulsive action he has seen as a lack in himself.

The trickster now becomes involved, as it very easily can, in collaboration with the shadow, rather than with the self. Once Hamlet abandons the caution that held him back, his shadow behavior takes over. Only once more does natural caution keep him from taking the king's life, when he finds him at prayers, and here his reasons are at least consciously born of vengeance, not his former hesitation.

His swift, horrible dispatch of Polonius would seem to confirm that position; that and the fact that it is easier to kill an enemy unseen than to look into his eyes. We see here also, in Hamlet's icy scorn, the cruelty of his hate for the old man, symbol of the false, bad father. When he remarks coldly that he took him for his better, the King, we are hearing not just a social convention but a still wistful loyalty toward his uncle, that shadow of his own father, for whom Polonius acts as scapegoat both psychologically and physically.

And now we come to Gertrude, the enigma who has been castigated far oftener than she has been defended. If we allow her to speak for herself, however, rather than viewing her through the eyes of Hamlet or another commentator, she emerges as a woman of compassion and great common sense.[15] Northrop Frye remarks that one of the problems with the play is that everyone, with the exception of the two women, talks too much.[16] Gertrude's remarks are scarce but unfailingly sensible and kind, veering toward impatience only with the exasperating Polonius. With Ophelia, she is motherly; with Rosencrantz and Guildenstern, warmly courteous; and with Hamlet, unquestionably loving. The scant conversations between her and Claudius suggest a warm, affectionate bond of understanding and trust, not the picture of unbridled lust Hamlet imagines.

Claudius and Gertrude are clearly in love. Looking at it from the viewpoint of psychological, rather than physical, reality, that is what kills Hamlet's father. Any replacement of a parent results in the psychological destruction of the *syzygy*, the wholeness of mother and father that is central to our archetypal expectations. Claudius has replaced the father and, in so doing, becomes the father and the arch enemy of the father all at once. Hamlet's ambivalence toward him is perfectly natural in that respect, but it is Gertrude's love for Claudius that provokes the most painful questions.

Did she love his father, as she seemed to, or was that merely an illusion? If she can love Claudius as much, then it calls into question both her character and that of his father, as well as the whole fabric of their union, the basis of Hamlet's existence. We have only to listen once more to Hamlet's description of his father to see the pathetic self-delusion there.

> See what a grace was seated on this brow:
> Hyperion's curls, the front of Jove himself,
> An eye like Mars, to threaten and command,
> A station like the herald Mercury
> New lighted on a [heaven] kissing hill,
> A combination and a form indeed,
> Where every god did seem to set his seal
> To give the world assurance of a man. (III.iv, 55-61)

A man indeed? This sounds more like a collage assembled from a child's illustrated book of mythology. Nowhere in Hamlet's description of his father can we detect an honest evaluation of the man.

What, then, might King Hamlet have been in reality? Have we any evidence to suggest that he was the father or the husband of his son's imagination, or was he merely a successful warrior, who held respect through fear? The furtive thought occurs to us, as it must to Hamlet, that possibly there was little difference between that godlike sire and his brother, the "mildewed ear." Or, worse yet, that Claudius, despite his faults, was the lesser of two evils, and that Gertrude's second marriage is a vast improvement over her first.

And so Hamlet, possessed by trickster/shadow, berates Gertrude and attempts to reconstitute her according to his expectations, as a sort of recycled virgin mother, "a queen, fair, sober, wise," and certainly celibate.

He leaves that shattering interview on a wistful note, expressing in the traditional Senecan *sentensia*, his bitter disappointment over the gulf between appearance and reality in his elders. Unceremoniously dragging the body of Polonius away, he remarks,

> This counsellor
> Is now most still, most secret, and most grave,
> Who was in life a foolish prating knave. (III.iv, 213-15)

Some of Shakespeare's blackest humor follows in the fourth act, when Hamlet's trickster engages in his verbal duel with the king concerning the whereabouts of Polonius. His famous reversal of the chain of being, characterizing kings as the food of worms, marks the height of his manic period. When next we see him, it is after he has seen Fortrinbras's army on the march, and his mood is sober once more.

Seeking truth, he reflects once more on what the world calls honor and determines that he will capitulate. But compare this speech with that of Henry V on the eve of the Battle of Agincourt. With what exquisite irony he exhorts himself to the cause! What Hamlet is this? Is it perhaps a variation of the earlier self-denouncer, still involved in shadow confusion? Or is it a sadly maturing ego, coming to terms at last with the absurdities of the world, of the collective shadow behavior that passes for logic and honor?

> Exposing what is mortal and unsure
> To all that fortune, death, and danger dare,
> Even for an egg shell. Rightly to be great
> Is not to stir without great argument,
> but greatly to find quarrel in a straw
> when honor's at the stake. (IV.iv, 51-56)

And finally he speaks, as in a trance, of the twenty thousand men who go to their graves, "for a fantasy and trick of fame." Then, vowing bloody thoughts or none, he leaves us to launch once more into the sea of the unconscious.

A few words here about Ophelia seem appropriate, as she makes her sad way down the path to madness and death. Her mad scene, so rarely played with the passion it deserves, is a vivid enactment of the drama of the rejected anima, plunged by misuse into self-destruction. The men in Ophelia's life have achieved an unplanned collaboration of devaluation that destroys her completely. The regard and love that she senses correctly from Hamlet have been destroyed by the cynicism of her father and brother. Hamlet then completes the job by his rejection of her and his murder of her father.

The bawdy songs that are so disturbing result form the men's sexual projections onto her. She feels soiled, stained, and irrevocably wounded because she has experienced the equivalent of a rape, when her sexual and spiritual innocence is brutally destroyed by not one, but three men. The murder of her father is the stroke that destroys her utterly, and that like the death of Hamlet's father, is a psychological as well as an actual event, because it represents the death of the idea as well as that of the man.

Thus Hamlet's anguished and rejected anima sinks back into the unconscious as Ophelia drowns in her flowery stream, not coincidentally at the time that he embarks upon his voyage into the unconscious once more.

Back to Gertrude, in a parenthetical comment here, as we observe her kindness toward Ophelia and her grief over the girl's death, both in the scene in which she gives Laertes the news and, later, at graveside. The graveside comment seems particularly pertinent, as Gertrude strews sweets to the sweet and mourns the bridal bed that is never to be. These are the words of a natural mother, one who wished happiness and love for the two young people, not the words of a wanton woman for whom loveless sexual license is a motivating factor. Gertrude, despite considerable opinion against her, never justifies that vilification, except by her unwise and overhasty marriage. She, like Ophelia, is to some extent at least a victim of male projection, both inside and outside the world of the play.

Now attention moves to Laertes, the sole survivor of his ill-favored family. In every respect he is the shadow of Hamlet, containing within himself all the qualities Hamlet does not display. While Hamlet has agonized for most of four acts, Laertes, untroubled by ambivalence, leads a charge of rabble against Claudius, attempting to find satisfaction in a coup. He wastes no time with facts when action is a possibility. Learning from Claudius the facts of Polonius's death, he falls easily into the poison plot, intent only on killing Hamlet however he can, even before the tragic news of Ophelia's death reaches him.

This, then, is the world's man that Hamlet cannot be: a man quick to anger who substitutes action for reason and to whom personal honor, or pride, is more important than justice. He does not, like Horatio, think and moderate his passion; he acts on it without reflection because action is not a result of, but a substitute for, thinking.

And so finally to the last act, where the jarring presence of the grave diggers pulls us out of the emotional maelstrom of the preceding scenes. But something far more important than the conventional comic relief at which Shakespeare is so adept is going on here. The trickster is back at his most earthy and irreverent, and he is not within Hamlet, nor do we ever see him there again but in the brief verbal skirmish with Osric, who represents all the falseness the true self most deplores. Hamlet's trickster is no longer in charge because he has been integrated on this last voyage into the unconscious. The death of Rosencrantz and Guildenstern symbolizes that integration. That clownish schoolboy pair, so lacking in substance or individuality, have to die if Hamlet is to leave his own boyhood behind. The regression caused by his double shock is over. He has mastered the demons that caused his stasis, and it is time to move on, not to the happy ending of fairy tales but to the mature realization that all life requires compromise. The dreams of childhood must fade in the cold, clear dawn of manhood.

Now the trickster appears in the far more appropriate guise of the grave diggers, and we are permitted briefly to enjoy, along with Horatio, the company of a man who has come to terms with himself.

The brief loss of control that plunges Hamlet into Ophelia's grave with Laertes is a fitting climax to the action, which moves inexorably toward its inevitable ending after that event. Symbolically, as he leaps into the grave, Hamlet becomes one with both Laertes and Ophelia. By publicly declaring his love he claims once more the rejected anima, and by his impulsive engagement with Laertes he finally integrates the elusive shadow qualities he has both fought and desired throughout the play, crying in bewilderment to Laertes,

> Hear you, sir,

> What is the reason that you use me thus?
> I lov'd you ever (V.i, 288-90)

Later, Hamlet's shadow integration continues, as he speaks to Horatio about his regrets at having "forgot himself" to Laertes, because the "bravery" of the other's grief put him into a "tow'ring passion." The untamed passion of Hamlet's shadow results from the imbalance in his thinking and feeling functions. Hamlet, sensitive and judicious, keeps himself under control except when under tremendous pressure, when the shadow qualities of his inferior function of feeling get the better of him. As a thinking intuitive, the prince sees what he perceives to be excessive emotion on Laertes's part, and his resultant discomfort propels him into a similar outburst.

The important issue here, however, is that Hamlet is beginning to understand these shadow qualities for what they are, to own them as part of himself, of his own humanity, rather than a suspect enemy to be destroyed.

Before the duel Hamlet apologizes directly to Laertes, insisting that it was "never Hamlet" but "Hamlet's madness" that is responsible for any wrongs to his friend. Hamlet can now look back on the trickster madness that gripped him, observing his former behavior as an outside spectator might do. He has, in a very real sense, come to himself now. He duels with Laertes as a matter of honor, allowing Laertes, the shadow, his opportunity to gain satisfaction for the many insults he has dealt him.

In a literal sense Hamlet is killed by his own shadow, Laertes. One conclusion from this line of thought might be that those shadow qualities he was unable to integrate are responsible for his death. That notion would dovetail quite neatly with what appears to be the pervasive critical opinion that Hamlet's hesitation is responsible for his tragic ending. A Laertes would surely have taken the ghost at his word, finished Claudius off, and gone on to the next adventure. Clearly that is the simple answer to this most complicated of puzzles.

But allow Laertes, the shadow, to speak for himself and the picture changes dramatically. He places the blame squarely on Claudius, pleading with his last breath,

> Exchange forgiveness with me, noble Hamlet.
> Mine and my father's death come not upon thee,

Nor thine on me! (V.ii, 329-31)

Hamlet is clearly reconciled with his shadow, the brave, impulsive, and rather ordinary Laertes.

Claudius, not Hamlet, must take responsibility for the evil and destruction around him. And who is Claudius but the shadow of his brother, Hamlet's father? Like Saturn, devouring his own children, the shadow of the father looms, unwilling to let go, determined to keep power at the expense of young lives.

This being true, why do we feel some satisfaction at the end of the play? What is this sense of triumph that permeates such a failure of good against bad? It is because Hamlet lives. Horatio, the self, does not die; only the ego, in its merger with the shadow, dies in the duel. Hamlet is transcendent, a miracle of rebirth amid the wreckage of life's unreconcilable opposites. This at once most gifted and most human of men has fought the battle for all of us and has shown us that there are no perfect solutions. Our mistakes are inevitable, because to err is human, and therein lies the remarkable solace of the play. Hamlet not only wavered for all of us; he died as a human sacrifice to the demands of the father. The Christian overtones are inescapable, and our pain at the injustice of all such acts is a deep and lasting wound for which this play provides a bitter but soothing balm.

Perhaps Hamlet, like all symbols of salvation, must die because of a primal fear still crouching somewhere deep within our collective psyche. Sir James Frazer reminds us in *The Golden Bough*:

> Primitive peoples . . . believe that their safety and even that of the world is bound up with the life of one of these god-men. . . . Naturally, therefore, they take the utmost care of his life. . . . But no amount of care and precaution will prevent the man-god from growing old and feeble. . . . There is only one way of averting these dangers. The man-god must be killed. The king is dead. Long live the king.[17]

When the militant young Fortinbras arrives, the symbol of self that legitimate authority invokes provides an assurance of continuity. His brief dialogue with Horatio, in which he speaks of the sorrow with which he embraces his fortune, gives us hope of the merger of these two symbols of the self: the thoughtful philosopher, Horatio, and the man of action, Fortinbras. For many the notion of Fortinbras as a manifestation of the self may prove difficult, but it is here that we return to the idea of Renaissance/medieval layering. Fortinbras never exists in this play at all, except as an emblem of the ruler, the man of war and action. Even Hamlet, the embodiment of man's attempt to civilize himself, must eventually act in ways that are in direct opposition to his own inclinations. So must we all at times, when placed in situations for which there is no good solution. Individuation does not mean perfection, but merely a striving toward the best of which each individual is capable, not in a vacuum, but in a world of conflict and confusion. Thus Hamlet lives in every civilized man and woman, in every thoughtful attempt to avoid violence as the ultimate solution. When he fails, we all fail, but he gives us courage, generation after generation, to attempt the ideal while existing with the sometimes nearly unbearable realities that life imposes.

Proceeding from the page to the stage we can see that another collaboration between Horatio and Fortinbras must take place within the director as scholar. The mountain of *Hamlet* criticism is matched by the dizzying variety of production and acting styles that have attempted to capture the essence of the play's meaning. How might they look to us now, that list of the theatre's elite who have breathed life into the Danish prince? The names alone are like a Who's Who of dramatic actors: Burbage, Betterton, Garrick, Kean, Booth, Bernhardt, Barrymore, Irving, Olivier, Gielgud, Redgrave, Burton, Jacobi, Kline, these few only begin to touch the surface.

Elsinore has been transformed into any number of things, including gangland Chicago of the twenties. A recent production[18] featured an unlikely but interesting Hamlet in Richard Thomas, who, along with an equally unlikely Gertrude (Pamela Payton-Wright) whose costume and demeanor suggested the present Queen Elizabeth, inhabited a postmodern world of plastic-covered battlements in process of repair and an unruly gaggle of broadcast journalists, ever ready to set up their electronic eyes and ears for the latest event in strife-torn Denmark.

Stratford, Ontario's most recent *Hamlet*[19] seemed to return to the nineteenth century for both scenography and acting style, presenting a Hamlet who ranted and declaimed in a manner that would have spoken more clearly to the Victorians than it does to contemporary audiences.

Still, each production and each performance adds, as does each critical analysis, to our common understanding of a treasure that will never be fully mined. From our Jungian perspective, nonetheless, one image emerges that seems to capture the essence of the melancholy prince, caught up in the trickster possession that so fascinates his critics and devotees. Imagine a figure bisected down the middle, like Harlequin, one side the jester, clad in motley, complete with cap, bells, and wand, the trickster in one of his most recognizable forms. Imagine, then, for the other half the traditional Hamlet, dressed in his inky cloak, the figure that has made its way into our collective imagination as the symbol of man's existential confusion.

"What a piece of work is man": light and dark, sublime and ridiculous, good and evil, wise and foolish, brave and cowardly, kind and cruel, sacred and profane. Shakespeare's mirror shows us the nature of man. We look into Hamlet's eyes and see ourselves. Jung allows us to look deeper, into the psyche, where the dark mirror clears and allows us to see our inner players face to face.

Chapter VI

Epilogue

Shakespeare's words, like all great art, speak to the intellect, the five senses, and to that least known part of ourselves, that "undiscovered country" of the unconscious mind. It is from that bourn that the traveler does return, somehow refreshed by the magic that has disappeared from our conscious world.

That other, unconscious world of myth and magic in which our ancestors lived their lives has been eroding slowly over the centuries, beginning its surge forward in the Renaissance, when the individual began to separate himself from the mass of mankind in large numbers.

Writing in 1928, in "The Spiritual Problem of Modern Man," Jung asserted, "He alone is modern who is fully conscious of the present," adding his own words to the body of work that explores and attempts to explain the alienation and the existential angst that continues to haunt the twentieth century. He categorizes any individual as "solitary"[1] who has managed to attain consciousness of the present. For him this is the hallmark of the "modern" man in all ages. Each step toward fuller consciousness becomes a step farther from the herd, from a purely animal "participation mystique," and from submersion in a common unconscious existence.

He categorizes any individual as "solitary" who has managed to attain consciousness of the present. For him this is the hallmark of the "modern" man in all ages. Each step toward fuller consciousness becomes a step farther from the herd, from a purely animal "participation mystique" and from submersion in a common unconscious existence.[2]

He goes on to suggest that this "modern" man of consciousness has existed historically, citing Jesus and Socrates as his examples. Shakespeare, a man both of and out of his time used the alchemy of art to connect those twin worlds of the conscious and the unconscious mind. In his plays, we see human reality as the recognizable tree of life whose many branches signify the myriad paths of man's experience that we can comprehend but dimly on the level of ordinary consciousness.

A contemporary American playwright, David Mamet, has defined the artist as "the dreamer of society,"[3] suggesting a sort of shaman who performs as a surrogate for a society that has lost its ability to connect with that other world or, perhaps more accurately, to reconcile those twin worlds of inner and outer experience.

Jung again:

> But what is significant in psychic life always lies below the horizon of consciousness, and when we speak of the spiritual problem of modern man we are speaking of things that are barely visible, of the most intimate and fragile things, of flowers that open only at night. In daylight everything is clear and tangible, but the night lasts as long as the day, and we live in the nighttime also. There are people who have bad dreams which even spoil their days for them. And for many people the day's life is such a bad dream that they long for the night when the spirit awakes.[4]

> Be not afeard; the isle is full of noises,
> Sounds, and sweet airs, that give delight
> and hurt not.
> Sometimes a thousand twangling instruments
> Will hum about mine ears; and sometime voices
> That, if I then had waked after long sleep,
> Will make me sleep again; and then, in
> dreaming,
> The clouds methought would open, and show
> riches

> Ready to drop upon me, that when I waked
> I cried to dream again. *The Tempest* (III.ii, 135-44)

Thus the Caliban within us all, our clumsy earthbound animal, dreams of things he understands but dimly when he wakes, and cries to dream again. The Prosperos among us, the Jungs and Shakespeares, work their magic to help us bring those dreams to consciousness as we learn to merge our inner and outer worlds.

It is my hope that this work will inspire others to explore Shakespeare's undiscovered country with the help of Jung's charts, and to find in that search still greater understanding of their genius and of our humanity.

Notes

Chapter I

1. Andrew Samuels et al., *A Critical Dictionary of Jungian Analysis* (New York: Routledge, 1986), 144-46.

2. Oscar G. Brockett, *History of the Theatre*, 4th ed. (Boston: Allyn & Bacon, 1982), chap. 1, "The Origins of Theatre."

3. C. G. Jung, *Four Archetypes:Mother/Rebirth/Spirit/ Trickster* (Princeton, N.J.: Bollingen, 1959), 47-81.

4. Charles Boyce, *Shakespeare A to Z: The Essential Reference to His Plays, His Poems, His Life and Times and More* (New York: Roundtable, 1990) 519.

5. Boyce, *Shakespeare A to Z*, 520.

6. Martyn Green, personal conversation with the author.

7. Harold C. Goddard, *The Meaning of Shakespeare* (Chicago: Phoenix, 1951), 332.

8. Samuels et al, *Dictionary*, 26-28.

Chapter II

1. James Kirsch, *Shakespeare's Royal Self* (New York: Putnam, 1966) Kirsch builds his thesis around this concept in discussing *Hamlet, King Lear and Macbeth.*

2. Bettina L. Knapp, *A Jungian Approach to Literature* (Carbondale: Southern Illinois University Press, 1984), 3-32.

3. W. S. Gilbert, *HMS Pinafore* (London: Brunswick, 1882)

4. Goddard, *Meaning*, 50-68.

5. Charlotte Spivack, *The Comedy of Evil on Shakespeare's Stage* (Cranbury: Associated University Presses, 1978), 83.

6. Katharina Wilson, *The Plays of Hrotsvit of Gandersheim* (New York: Garland, 1989). All the plays, particularly *Sapientia*, deal with this theme.

7. Edward F. Edinger, *Ego and Archetype* (Baltimore: Penguin, 1973), Edinger devotes much of the book to the process of inflation and alienation that characterizes the development of the individual.

8. C. G. Jung, *Man and his Symbols* (New York: Doubleday, 1964), 198.

9. C. G. Jung, *The Portable Jung*, ed. Joseph Campbell. (New York: Penguin, 1971), 153.

10. Sally Porterfield, "Little Girl Lost and Little Girl Found: The Role of the Animus in *Wuthering Heights* and *Jane Eyre*", paper read at the NEMLA conference Hartford, Connecticut, spring 1991.

11. Jung, *Portable*, 155.

12. Ibid.

13. Peter Brook, *The Shifting Point*, (New York: Harper & Row, 1987), 135-156. Brook discusses production elements of the play.

14. Christopher Durang, *Sister Mary Ignatius Explains It All for You* (New York: Doubleday, 1981). Durang provides a savagely funny example of this phenomenon.

15. Brook, *The Empty Space* (New York: Atheneum, 1984) 89.

16. Joseph Papp's American Shakespeare Festival production, directed by mark Lamos at the Mitzi Gaynor Theatre, in New York, 1989. The Duke played by Len Cariou.

17. Goddard, *Meaning* 65.

Chapter III

1. G. Balkemore Evans et al., *The Riverside Shakespeare* (Boston: Houghton Mifflin, 1974), 445.

2. Jung, *Portable*, "Concept of a Collective Psyche," 65.

3. Knapp, *Jungian Approach*, 113-25.

4. Janet Adelman, "This Is and Is Not Cressid," in *The (M)other Tongue: Essays in Feminist Psychoanalytic Interpretation*, ed. Shirley Nelson Garner et al. (Ithaca, N.Y.: Cornell University Press, 1985), 119-41.

5. Robin Morgan, *The Demon Lover: On the Sexuality of Terrorism* (New York: Norton, 1989), 181-91.

6. Sitansu Maitra, *Psychological Realism and Archetypes: The Trickster in Shakespeare* (Calcutta: Bookland, 1967), 120-21.

7. Boyce, *Shakespeare A to Z*, 7.

8. Adelman, "Cressid," 119-41.

9. Boyce, *Shakespeare A to Z*, 5.

10. June Singer, "Jung's Gnosticism and Contemporary Gnosis," in *Jung's Challenge to Contemporary Religion*, (Wilmette, Ill: Chiron, 1987), 73-91.

11. Jung, *Four Archetypes*, 85-131.

12. Demaris S. Wehr, *Jung and Feminism: Liberating Archetypes* (Boston: Beacon, 1987). A succinct and helpful discussion of the inherent sexism in Jung's theories, and the ways in which they can be expanded to embrace societal changes.

Chapter IV

1. Evans, *Riverside*, 499-503.

2. Mary Rodgers, *Once Upon a Mattress* (New York: Chappell, 1959).

3. Boyce, *Shakespeare A to Z*, 61.

4. Jolande Jacobi, *The Way of Individuation* (Ontario: Signet, 1965), 27-28.

5. Jung, *Four Archetypes*, 135-152.

6. Ibid., 140.

7. Ibid., 152.

8. John Beebe, "The Trickster in the Arts," *San Francisco Jung Institute Library Journal*, 2 no. 2 (1981), 22.

9. Nancy Chodorow, as quoted by Coppellia Kahn, "The Hand That Rocks the Cradle," in *The (M)other Tongue*, 77.

10. C. G. Jung and C. Kerenyi, *Essays on a Science of Mythology* (Princeton, N.J.: Bollingen, 1973), 137.

11. Russel A. Fraser and Norman Rabkin, *Drama of the English*

Renaissance, vol. 1: *The Tudor Period* vol. 2: *The Stuart Period* (New York: Macmillan, 1976). The custom of setting tragedies and, thus, villains in foreign countries was widely practiced by Shakespeare and his contemporaries, as witnessed by Thomas Kyd's prototypical work, *The Spanish Tragedy*. The custom continued throughout the Jacobean period with Webster, Jonson, and Ford.

Chapter V

1. Quoted in Boyce, *Shakespeare A to Z*, 236.

2. Ernest Jones, "The Death of Hamlet's Father," in *Literature & Psychoanalysis*, ed. Edith Kurzwell and William Phillips (New York: Columbia University Press, 1983), 34-38.

3. D. W. Winnicott, *Playing and Reality*. (New York: Routledge, 1971), 10-12.

4. Goddard, *Meaning*, 359.

5. Jung, "On the Psychology of the Trickster-Figure," in *Four Archetypes*, 135-52.

6. Goddard, *Meaning*, 162.

7. Jung, *Four Archetypes*, 94.

8. Anthony Stevens, *Archetypes: A Natural History of the Self* (London: Routledge, 1982). Stevens deals with the concept of societal archetypes throughout the book, in which he argues for an ethological approach to archetypal patterns.

9. Goddard, *Meaning*, 345.

10. Ibid., 345.

11. Ibid., 342.

12. Emily Dickinson in a letter to Mrs. T. W. Higginson, summer 1877. "Dear friend, I send you a flower from my garden. Though it die in reaching you, you will know it lived when it left my hand. Hamlet wavered for all of us." Thomas H. Johnson and Theodora Ward, eds., *The Letters of Emily Dickinson* (Cambridge: Belknap University Press, 1958).

13. Jane Wagner, *The Search for Intelligent Life in the Universe*. Performance by Lily Tomlin in N.Y., (1986).

14. Goddard, *Meaning*, 367.

15. Carolyn G. Heilbrun, *Hamlet's Mother and Other Women* (New York: Columbia University Press, 1990), 1-17.

16. Northrop Frye, *Northrop Frye on Shakespeare* (New Haven:

Yale University Press, 1986), 83.

17. Sir James Frazer, *The Golden Bough* (New York: Macmillan, 1950), 309.

18. Hartford Stage Company, directed by Mark Lamos, 1990.

19. Stratford, Ontario, Shakespeare Festival, 1991.

Epilogue

1. Jung, *Portable*, 456.

2. Ibid.

3. Quoted in Mark Lamos, "Reflections from the Artistic Director," in program for *The Painful Adventures of Pericles, Prince of Tyre* at the Hartford Stage Company, February 15 - March 21, 1987.

4. Jung, *Portable*, 472.

Bibliography

Armens, Sven. *Archetypes of the Family in Literature*. Seattle: University of Washington Press, 1966.

Aronson, Alex. *Psyche & Symbol in Shakespeare*. Bloomington: Indiana University Press, 1977.

Beebe, John. "The Trickster in the Arts." *San Francisco Jung Institute Library Journal* 2, no. 2 (1981), 22-54.

Bodkin, Maud. *Archetypal Patterns in Poetry: Psychological Studies of Imagination.* London: Oxford University Press, 1934.

Boe, John. "To Kill Mercutio." *Quadrant: Notes on Analytical Psychology* 8, no. 2 (1975), 97-105.

Boyce, Charles. *Shakespeare A to Z: The Essential Reference to His Plays, His Poems, His Life and Times and More.* New York: Roundtable, 1990.

Brockett, Oscar G. *History of the Theatre.* 4th ed. Boston: Allyn & Bacon, 1982.

Brook, Peter. *The Empty Space.* New York: Atheneum, 1984.

--- *The Shifting Point.* New York: Harper & Row, 1987.

Campbell, Joseph. *The Hero with a Thousand Faces.* Princeton N.J.: Bollingen, 1973.

Chaikin, Joseph. *The Presence of the Actor: Notes on The Open Theatre, Disguises, Acting and Repression.* New York: Atheneum, 1984.

Cohen, Robert. *The Theatre.* 2nd ed. California: Mayfield, 1988.

Coursen, H. R. "Age Is Unnecessary: A Jungian Approach to *King Lear.*" Bowdoin College, (periodical info. missing).

Driscoll, James P. *Identity in Shakespearean Drama.* Lewisburg, PA: Bucknell University Press, 1988.

Edinger, Edward F. *Ego and Archetype.* Baltimore: Penguin, 1973.

Elsom, John. ed. *Is Shakespeare Still Our Contemporary?* London: Routledge, 1989.

Evans, G. Blakemore, et al., eds. *The Riverside Shakespeare.* Boston: Houghton Mifflin, 1974.

Fraser, Russell A., and Norman Rabkin. *Drama of the English Renaissance. Vol. 1: The Tudor Period* and Vol. 2: The Stuart Period. New York: Macmillan, 1976.

Frazer, Sir James George. *The Golden Bough.* New York: Macmillan, 1922.

Freud, Sigmund. *A General Selection from the Works of Sigmund Freud.* Edited by John Rickman, M.D. New York: Norton, 1937.

---. *On Dreams.* James Strachey, ed. New York: Norton, 1952.

---. *The Ego and the Id.* Edited by James Strachey New York: Norton, 1960.

---. *An Outline of Psycho-Analysis.* Edited by James Strachey New York: Norton, 1969.

French, Marilyn. *Shakespeare's Division of Experience.* London: Abacus, 1982.

Frey-Rohn, Liliane. *From Freud to Jung.* Boston: Shambala, 1990.

Frye, Northrop. *Anatomy of Criticism.* Princeton N.J.: Princeton University Press, 1958.

---. *Northrop Frye on Shakespeare.* New Haven: Yale University Press, 1986.

Garner, Shirley Nelson, Claire Kahane, Sprengnether, and Madelon, eds. *The (M)other Tongue: Essays in Feminist Psychoanalytic Interpretation.* Ithaca N.Y.: Cornell University Press, 1985.

Gilbert, W.S. *HMS Pinafore.* London: Brunswick, 1882.

Goddard, Harold C. *The Meaning of Shakespeare.* Chicago: Phoenix, 1951.

Heilbrun, Carolyn G. *Hamlet's Mother and Other Women.* New York: Columbia, 1990.

Hillman, James. *A Blue Fire.* New York: Harper & Row, 1989.
Holland, Norman. *Psychoanalysis & Shakespeare.* New York: McGraw-Hill, 1964.
Holtzberger, William G., and Peter B. Waldeck, eds. *Perspective on Hamlet.* Lewisburg PA: Bucknell University Press, 1975.
Isbister, J. *Freud: An Introduction to His Life and Work.* Cambridge England: Polity Press, 1985.
Jacobi, Jolande. *The Way of Individuation.* Ontario: Signet, 1965.
Johnson, Thomas H., and Theodora Ward, eds. *The Letters Emily Dickinson.* Cambridge: Belknap Press of Harvard University, 1958.
Jung, C. G. *Answer to Job.* Princeton, N.J.: Bollingen, 1958.
---. *Psyche & Symbol.* Edited by Violet S. de Laszlo. New York: Doubleday, 1958.
---. *The Basic Writings of C. G. Jung.* Edited by Violet S. de Laszlo. New York: Modern Library, 1959.
---. *Four Archetypes: Mother/Rebirth/Spirit/Trickster.* Princeton, N.J.: Bollingen, 1959.
---. *Man and His Symbols.* New York: Doubleday, 1964.
---. *The Portable Jung.* Edited by Joseph Campbell. New York: Penguin, 1971.
---. *Memories, Dreams, Reflections.* New York: Vintage, 1989.
Jung, C. G., and C. Kerenyi. *Essays on a Science of Mythology.* Princeton, N.J.: Bollingen, 1973.
Kerr, Walter. *Journey to the Center of the Theatre.* New York: Knopf, 1979.
Kirsch, James. *Shakespeare's Royal Self.* New York: Putnam, 1966.
Knapp, Bettina L. *A Jungian Approach to Literature.* Carbondale: Southern Illinois University Press, 1984.
Kott, Jan. *Shakespeare Our Contemporary.* New York: Norton, 1966.
Kurzweil, Edith and William Phillips, eds. *Literature & Psychoanalysis.* New York: Columbia University Press, 1983.
Lamos, Mark. "Reflections from the Artistic Director." Program for *The Painful Adventures of Pericles, Prince of Tyre* at the Hartford
Stage Company. Feb 15 - March 21, 1987.
Lenz, Carolyn Ruth Swift, Gayle Greene, Carol Thomas Neely. *The Woman's part: Feminist Criticism of Shakespeare.* Chicago:

University of Chicago, 1983.

Maitra, Sitansu. *Psychological Realism and Archetypes: The Trickster in Shakespeare*. Calcutta: Bookland, 1967.

Morgan, Robin. *The Demon Lover: on the Sexuality of Terrorism*. New York: Norton, 1989.

Nagler, A. M. *A Source Book in Theatrical History*. Toronto: General Publishing, 1952.

Neumann, Erich. *Amor & Psyche: The Psychic Development of the Feminine*. New York: Bollingen, 1956.

Porterfield, Sally. "Little Girl Lost and Little Girl Found: The Role of the Animus in *Jane Eyre* and *Wuthering Heights*." NEMLA conference in Hartford Connecticut, Spring, 1991.

Samuels, Andrew. *Jung and the Post Jungians*. New York: Routledge and Kegan Paul, 1985.

Samuels, Andrew, Bani Shorter, and Fred Plant. *A Critical Dictionary of Jungian Analysis*. New York: Routledge, 1986.

Scott, W.I.D. *Shakespeare's Melancholics*. London: Mills & Boon, 1962.

Shakespeare, William. *The Riverside Shakespeare*. Boston: Houghton Mifflin, 1974.

Singer, June. *Boundaries of the Soul: The Practice of Jung's Psychology*. New York: Anchor Doubleday, 1972.

Speaight, Robert. *Shakespeare on the Stage*. Boston: Little, Brown, 1973.

Spivack, Charlotte. *The Comedy of Evil on Shakespeare's Stage*. Cranbury: Associated University Presses, 1978.

Stein, E. Murray and Robert L. Moore. *Jung's Challenge to Contemporary Religion*. Wilmette, Ill: Chiron, 1987.

Sternlicht, Irwin R. "Shakespeare and the Feminine." In *A Well of Living Waters: A Festschrift for Hilde Kirsch*. Edited by Rhoda Head, Rose-Emily Rothenberg, and David Wesley. Los Angeles: Jung Institute, 1977, 189-203.

Stevens, Anthony. *Archetypes: A Natural History of the Self*. London: Routledge, 1982.

---. *On Jung*. London: Routledge and Kegan Paul, 1990.

Van Meurs, Jos, with John Kidd. *Jungian Literary Criticism, 1920-1980: An Annotated, Critical Bibliography of Works in English (With a Selection of Titles after 1980)*. Metuchen, N.J., & London: Scarecrow Press, 1988.

Volker, Klaus. *Brecht: A Biography*. New York: Seabury, 1978.
Wehr, Demaris S. *Jung and Feminism: Liberating Archetypes*. Boston: Beacon, 1987.
Wilson, Katharina. *The Plays of Hrotsvit of Gandersheim*. New York: Garland, 1989.
Winnicott, D. W. *Playing and Reality*. New York: Routledge, 1971.

Index

About the Author

SALLY F. PORTERFIELD teaches and directs at the Hartt School at the University of Hartford and the University of Connecticut. She has also been a working theatre critic and free-lance writer for 20 years.

ISBN 0-313-29305-8
90000>
EAN
9 780313 293054
HARDCOVER BAR CODE